THE HIDDEN HISTORY OF THE SINO-INDIAN FRONTIER

MINERVA ASSOCIATES (PUBLICATIONS) PVT. LTD.
7-B, Lake Place : Calcutta-700-029

© Karunakar Gupta, 1974

First published : August, 1974

ISBN : 0-88386-438-X

Printed in India by M. K. Mukerjee at Temple Press, 2, Nayaratna Lane, Calcutta-700 004 and published by T. K. Mukherjee for and on behalf of Minerva Associates (Publications) Pvt. Ltd., 7-B, Lake Place, Calcutta-700 029.

The Hidden History of the Sino-Indian Frontier

KARUNAKAR GUPTA

INDIA

INTRODUCTION

I

Sino-Indian friendship was one of the main planks of Nehru's foreign policy. "A powerful neighbour is a potential enemy" is a saying as old as Kautilya. But the leaders of India as well as Communist China developed sympathies between themselves, having suffered a common experience of White colonialism for more than a century, despite their divergent ideologies. Even in the context of the decision of Communist China to establish its hegemony over Tibet in the autumn of 1950,—although Tibet had enjoyed the status of a buffer-state between British India and China for about forty years—Nehru accepted the change gracefully in the context of the new balance of power in Asia, when China had proved her prowess against the U.S. army under the U.N. flag in the battlefield of Korea. Nehru said in a radio speech in London on 13 January 1951 : "China, in her new-found strength, has acted sometimes in a manner which I deeply regret. But we have to remember the background of China, as of other Asian countries —the long period of struggle and frustration, the insolent treatment that they received from the imperialist powers and the latter's refusal to deal with them in terms of equality. It is neither right nor practical to ignore the feelings of hundreds of millions of people. It is no longer safe to do so." The American refusal to extend recognition to Communist China, the American intervention in North Korea, Formosa and the threat of nuclear attack on Vietnam—as also the U.S. military aid to Pakistan—enhanced the danger of a new war in Asia. In this context, Nehru wanted to ensure peace and stability in Asia through Sino-Indian co-operation. In the Sino-Indian Treaty on Tibetan Trade and Pilgrimage of April 1954, India readily gave up the extra-territorial rights in Tibet, exercised by the British Raj on the basis of the secret Anglo-Tibetan Trade Agreements of July 1914, whose legal validity was doubtful. The negotiations leading to the signing of the Sino-Indian Trade Agreement of April 1954 provided adequate indication to Nehru that Communist China might be prepared to acquiesce in the Indian claim to the MacMahon Line. Also India, for the first time, secured the right of establishing a permanent Consulate-General in Lhasa—which would provide a good listening post for gathering information about the developments in the extensive Trans-Himalayan plateau. China's tacit acceptance of the Indian take-over of Tawang in February 1951 and her ommission to raise the issue of India's frontier activities in NEFA area at the Conference table in Peking, convinced Nehru about the conciliatory attitude of Communist China towards India's desire to reach up to the Himalayan crest line i.e., the MacMahon Line and make it the *de facto* boundary. This was quite in contrast with the attitude of Nationalist China, which had officially challenged the validity of Indo-Tibetan Border Agreement of July 1914. On the other hand, India's diplomatic support to China on various international issues in the U.N. and other international Conferences strengthened the foundations of friendship between India and China during the early fifties.

II

The main theme of this book is to present how the feeling of resurgent Asianism—which animated both India and China in the fifties and brought them closer in the face of enormous tasks of rapid national reconstruction—was destroyed by the operation of certain complex factors and coincidence of events. As early as 1950-51, Nehru wrote to Sir B. N. Rau, our envoy in the United Nations during the days of the Korean War : "I see that both the United States and the U.K. on the one hand and the U.S.S.R. on the other, for entirely different reasons, are not anxious that India and China should be friendly towards one another. That itself is a significant fact which was to be borne in mind." (Nehru and the U.N. during the Korean Crisis, *The Statesman,* 7 December 1965).

Apart from the Great Powers, there were other alien forces who were working to undermine Sino-Indian solidarity by using India herself as the base of their anti-Chinese activities. There has been a powerful Taiwan lobby operating in the Himalayan border regions of India, which was acting in close co-operation with the disgruntled Tibetan nobles, most of whom found their haven in Kalimpong after the establishment of the Communist regime in China. Perhaps the most influential personality representing both the Taiwan lobby and the Tibetan lobby based in India has been Gyalu Thondup, one of the elder brothers of the Dalai Lama, who was educated in the Whampoa Military Academy, and married to a Chinese lady of high birth related to General Chiang Kai-shek. According to Professor A. R. Field, the foundation of Nationalist Chinese intelligence net in Tibet was set up by Gyalu Thondup. Gyalu Thondup shifted his establishment from Tibet to India in the wake of the Communist revolution in China. Gyalu Thondup has been very active among the Tibetan exiles living in India as a champion of Tibetan independence and his activities earned him the ire of the Communist Government of China, so much so that they asked the Government of India for his externment, in an official Note in July 1958. George Patterson, who has been an open champion of the cause of Tibetan independence, reveals in his book *Tibet In Revolt* (pp. 152-153), that Gyalu Thondup played an important part in drawing up the manifesto of Tibetan independence at a meeting of Tibetan rebels (including members of Dalai Lama's Cabinet and guerrilla leaders from the Khampa areas bordering on Tibet) which was held in Kalimpong on 4 August 1958. The name of Gyalu Thondup cropped again and again in the press in connection with the efforts of the Tibetan freedom-fighters to draw support from world community. The style of his living, his several trips to Taiwan, the U.S.A. and Europe since he set up his establishment in India in 1950, indicated that Gyalu was involved in the game of China-baiting at a very high level. His close personal connections with some key officials of the Government of India during the fifties—such as Apa Pant, the Political Officer in Sikkim, and B. N. Mullik, the chief of Intelligence Bureau—would partially explain why the Government of India failed to comply with the request of the Government of China to discontinue his residence permit in India during all these years. The Government of Bhutan has recently brought to light certain facts which reveal clearly the obnoxious nature of anti-China activities of certain Tibetan exiles across the Himalayan borders, allegedly committed under the inspiration of Gyalu Thondup. For many years, the Dalai Lama had been very much under the spell of his elder brother Gyalu, and during all these years since India granted him political asylum in April 1959, he had been encouraged to make political speeches against the Communist Government of China, invoking the aid to the USA, the UK, and the Western World, for the redemption of Tibetan freedom —thus violating the very conditions of "Political asylum". (This has been a continuing cause of Sino-Indian misunderstanding since 1959. On 25 April 1950, Chou En-lai made this point clear at his press conference in New Delhi). The recent speeches of the Dalai Lama, appreciating the merits of Soviet Communism, indicate that the Tibetan leaders in exile are now trying to fish in the troubled waters of Sino-Soviet impasse, after having made capital of the Sino-American impasse during more than two decades as also having received the support of the entire Western World.

It has been one of my contentions that the leaders of Tibet played a major role in vitiating Sino-Indian relations since the fifties—of course with the clandestine support they received from the various Western agencies, particularly the C.I.A. In this respect we can aptly quote the comment of K. Zilliacus : "It is the nemesis of Power Politics that it begins by Great Powers making pawns of small states and ends in small states using the rivalries of the Great Powers to serve their ends." For too long, the Tibetan leaders have been sitting tight over the shoulders of the Government of India like the Old Man in the story of Sindbad—the Sailor in the *Arabian Nights,* taking advantage of the Sino-Indian impasse, which has resulted in the enormous arms burden on both sides and harmed the cause of the Third World solidarity against the pressure of the Affluent world. Some leaders of Pakistan, Nepal, Kashmir, Bhutan and Sikkim etc. also had a sense of vested interest in the perpetuation of the Sino-Indian stalemate from which they reaped material benefits.

It is also necessary to mention here the doings of some British Officials of the days of the Raj, who had been following the precept—"Let the Asians fight the Asians"—long before it was enunciated by Dulles in America. A study of the career of Sir Olaf Caroe would show that this formidable scholar, who had served as the Foreign Secretary of India under the British Raj during 1939-1945, was a vehement critic of Nehru's policy of non-alignment tinged with anti-colonialism, and tried to bolster up Pakistan as against India by pleading in favour of military aid to Pakistan with high level State Department officials in the U.S.A. in 1951. While serving in New Delhi, he arranged in 1938 the publication of a spurious version of *Aitchison's Treaties* relating to Tibet, suppressing the original edition. His purpose was to falsely assert that the abortive tripartite Simla Conference of 1913-1914 was a partial success and that it fixed the North-eastern frontier of India along the Himalayan crest line. i.e. the MacMahon Line by a bilateral Anglo-Tibetan declaration while the Sino-Tibetan boundary line could not be settled due to Chinese intransigence. In 1945, under Caroe's guidance, Hugh Richardson produced an official handbook known as *Tibetan precis,* in which again the false story was repeated that the Simla Conference sanctified the Indo-Tibetan boundary along the Himalayan crest-line. Though it remained forgotten for some years because of World War I, it was re-discovered and efforts were made to make the Frontier a reality in late thirties. These two official documents proved to be two veritable time-bombs causing a violent rupture in Sino-Indian relations in the wake of the Tibetan uprising and the flight of the Dalai Lama to India in April 1959. It was an irony of history that when the India-China border dispute became an open issue since September 1959, the Government of India sought the help of Sir Olaf Caroe to argue its case for the MacMahon Line. Writing on the subject in the *Manchester Guardian,* dated 13 February 1960, Caroe repeated the arguments incorporated in the concocted version of the *Aitchison's Treaties* relating to Tibet produced by himself and emphasised that the MacMahon Line had the same legal validity as of the Durand Line which fixed the boundary between British India and Afghanistan. Sir Alaf Caroe paid a visit to India in the Fall of 1963, on the invitation of the Government of India for the ostensible purpose of advising them on the problem of Tibetan refugees settled in India. Reportedly, it was on his advice that the Government of India absorbed a large number of Tibetan exiles in manning the frontier posts along the whole stretch of the Himalayan frontiers after giving them necessary military training. This has been an act of gross diplomatic blunder on the part of India, which has been reciprocated by China giving support to the irredentist minority leaders of Kashmir, Nagaland, Mizoram etc. and may prove to be a stumbling block towards Sino-Indian rapprochement. Neville Maxwell informs us, "B. J. Patnaik was given responsibilities in recruiting and training Tibetan refugees for guerrilla action in their homeland" (*India's China War*, p. 440). George Patterson also refers to the recruitment of large number of Tibetans for fighting with the Indian forces in any future war with China. (*Peking versus Delhi* : p. 166).

Now we may refer to the role of the Soviet Union in the continuing stalemate in Sino-Indian relations. According to Mohan Ram, the Sino-Indian dispute is but a function of the more complicated Sino-Soviet dispute and it is futile to expect a normalisation of India-China relations until there is a *detenté* in Sino-Soviet relations. Comparing the nature of China's border disputes with her two big neighbours, Professor Alastair Lamb wrote, "While on the Sino-Russian border it is probable that border problems have been aggravated by international tension rather than the other way about, there were good grounds for believing that on the Sino-Indian border it was the failure to solve border problems that produced a crisis in international relations. (The Sino-Indian and Sino-Russian Borders in *Studies in Social History of China and South-East Asia*, edited by J. Ch'en & Tarling, 1970). Since the Tass *Communique* dated 9 September 1959, the Soviet leaders have been from time to time making open statements relating to the continuing Sino-Indian border dispute. For a long time, the Soviet Union chose to be benevolently neutral on the respective border claims. Nehru and Krishna Menon, however, sought to make a capital of this Soviet neutrality, pointing out that it was first occasion since 1917 that the Soviet Union had taken a neutral position in a dispute between a Communist country and a non-Communist country. The Chinese documents relating to the sources of the Sino-Soviet dispute also make a bitter reference to the Tass communiqué of September 1959, for bringing into the open the first time the rift within the World Communism.

On the other hand, the Soviet maps had been showing the Sino-Indian borders more or less in conformity with the Chinese claims, and this caused great annoyance and chagrin in New Delhi from time to time. As a Moscow-based correspondent wrote in *Far Eastern Economic Review,* 17 June 1974, "For a decade after the Sino-Indian war of 1962, Moscow refused to commit itself on the merit of the border claims, although Soviet criticism of China's policy towards India became more and more outspoken and frequent." Even the signing of the Indo-Soviet Treaty on 3 August, 1971, did not immediately alter the Soviet view on the Sino-Indian border claims. But in December 1972, the newly started Russian Quarterly journal *Prob. Dalnevo Rostoka* (Far Eastern Affairs), published a lengthy study of the history of the Chinese policy towards the Indian sub-continent in the late fifties and early sixties, which was remarkable for its Indo-centric views on the Sino-Indian border dispute. In the March 1974 issue of this journal of Soviet academicians, the editors have chosen to publish a bitterly critical review article on Neville Maxwell's four-year old book, *India's China War* (1970). The timing of this Soviet article seems to be no less significant than its contents. It came out at a time, when India was being strongly buffeted by the cross-currents of big power rivalry and attention. The Soviet Union since the recent past has been apparently gravely concerned that a reconciliation between Peking and New Delhi might be brought on terms inimical to her power interests in South Asia and in the present state of Sino-Soviet Cold War. Soviet diplomacy might be expected to be active in preventing the progress of a Sino-Indian *detenté*. This is perhaps the only way that one can explain the anti-Chinese statements relating to the Sino-Indian border dispute made by several dignitaries from the Soviet world during their recent visit to India.

Whatever may be the attitude of the world powers towards a Sino-Indian rapprochement, it is in the vital interests of both India and China to resolve their 15-year old dispute, which had hardly any deep ideological element in it, unlike the Sino-Soviet dispute.

The main framers of our foreign policy in the early days such as Nehru, Krishna Menon and K. P. S. Menon agreed on the point that the tremendous frontier along the high Himalayas which we share with China has to be tackled in a peaceful way. They knew well Lord Curzon's dictum "the frontiers are indeed the razor's edge on which hang suspended the modern issues of war or peace, of life or death to nation." The solution they looked to was the creation of a frontier of peace and friendship along the Himalayas like the Canada-America frontier. Also they knew that it could be achieved only by a conciliation between the concept of Tibetan autonomy and Chinese sovereignty. It would be relevant to mention here that on the Chinese side also at least one outstanding scholar gave serious thought to the complexity of the Sino-Indian frontier problem and came to a similar conclusion : "Whatever the world situation proves to be. . . . an understanding between China and India such as exists between United States and Canada, with an agreement to de-militarize the Himalayas, which are the controlling factors of both Indian and Chinese geography, would not be only a guarantee to the autonomous status of Tibet but also a stabilising factor in the peace of the world." (*Tibet To-day and Yesterday*, p. 217; T. T. Li, 1960).

III

During 1950-1953, Korea became the battle-ground between the armies of the Western Bloc (led by the U.S.A.) fighting under the banner of the U.N. and the armies of the Communist Bloc represented by the North Koreans and the Chinese, while the U.S.S.R. became their arsenal. The war in Korea, though looked upon as a "limited war" by the West, was considered by Nehru as the third greatest war in history. The U.S.A. sustained 142,000 casualties, Commonwealth troops suffered 7,000 casualties, the Turks 3,000. These were inconsiderable compared with the huge losses suffered by the Chinese and the Koreans. According to J. F. Dulles, ten million people were killed in North Korea alone. For a serious student of Nehru's foreign policy, a close study of the Korean crisis is essential. As K.P.S. Menon wrote, "It was Korea which first impressed the grim realities of Cold War on India. India had been independent for barely four months, when she was appointed as a Member of the U.N. Commission on Korea and was elected Chairman. It was in connection with Korea that India, in turn, impressed the world with the reality of the policy of non-alignment."

The importance of the study of the origin of the Korean War for the students of Far Eastern international relations will be clear from the following comment of Edgar Snow made in 1963 : "To this day the Peking Government maintains—and most of the people of China seem to believe—that South Korea began the attack at American instigation. I have seen no convincing proof of that, I do not believe it, and most of the world does not believe it. *(If it should ever be proved more than a decade of history would have to be completely rewritten.)*" *(The Other side of The River,* p. 714).

The article, "Origin of the Korean War and India's stand", was published in June 1956 in the *Calcutta Review*. Therein, I called for the setting up of a Neutral Investigation Commission to investigate into the origin of the Korean War under an Indian Chairman. This comment lost its relevance since July 1958, when India's role as a mediator became suspect in China's eyes—mainly due to the hostile operations of the Tibetan exiles in India.

CONTENTS

	PAGE
INTRODUCTION	V

PART I:

The Hidden History of the Sino-Indian Frontier	3
Sino-Indian Relations (1947-59)—A Retrospect	36
The Sino-Indian Dispute	51
Sino-Indian Relations—The Prospects of a Detenté	55
The MacMahon Line: From a Myth towards Reality	62
The North-East Frontier of India: The British Legacy	66
Sardar K. M. Panikkar and the Formative Phase of Indian Foreign Policy	97

PART II:

The Korean Crisis and the United Nations	107
A New Look into the Origin of the Korean War	114
Origin of the Korean War and India's Stand	152
Appendix	163
Index	174

PART I

1. THE HIDDEN HISTORY OF THE SINO-INDIAN FRONTIER
2. SINO-INDIAN RELATIONS—A RETROSPECT
3. THE SINO-INDIAN DISPUTE
4. SINO-INDIAN RELATIONS—THE PROSPECTS OF A DETENTÉ
5. THE MCMAHON LINE : FROM A MYTH TOWARDS REALITY
6. THE NORTH-EAST FRONTIER OF INDIA : THE BRITISH LEGACY
7. SARDAR K. M. PANIKKAR AND THE FORMATIVE PHASE OF INDIAN FOREIGN POLICY

PART II

THE HIDDEN HISTORY OF THE
SINO-INDIAN FRONTIER (1947—1959)

"In International politics, the habit of saying one thing and thinking another is as old as time". (Lord Birdwood : A Continent Decides)

I

There has been complete ignorance among large sections of the Indian public regarding the truth of the British legacy about the Northern frontier. The Survey of India maps published in free India during 1947-1952 depicted the North-eastern border of India, eastward from Bhutan, along the Himalayan high-crest line as 'undemarcated', while the Western sector and the middle sector of the Northern border beginning from the North-western end of Kashmir to the tri-junction of Nepal-Tibet-India were shown by a colour-wash with the words 'Boundary Undefined' imprinted thrice along the stretch. In the authoritative publication of the Foreign and Political Department of the British Government of India—generally known as *Aitchison's Treaties* — relating to Kashmir, it was written explicitly, "The northern as well as the eastern boundary of the Kashmir State is still undefined." (Vol. XII Part I p. 5, 1931).

The Indian public never bothered about the 'Undefined Boundary' along the Kashmir sector, because the Government of India had been declaring from time to time since October 1947 that the future of Kashmir would be finally decided through a U.N.-supervised plebiscite after the withdrawal of the invaders coming from the Pakistan territory. The Indian attitude towards the future of Kashmir gradually hardened since the signing of the Pak-American military aid agreement in February 1954. But even then, we find that in a resolution adopted as late as 2nd December, 1957, the U.N. Security Council took cognizance of the fact that the Governments of both India and Pakistan did "recognize and accept the provisions of its resolution dated 17th January, 1948, and resolutions of the U.N. Commission for India and Pakistan dated 13th August, 1948 and 5th January, 1949, which envisage in accordance with their terms the determination of the future status of the State of Kashmir in accordance with the will of the people through the democratic method of a free and impartial plebiscite." This would at least partially explain why Nehru did not raise any point of dispute about the Kashmir frontier specifically either when he visited Peking in October, 1954, or later in the winter of 1956-1957 when Chou En-lai paid visits to India. A close scrutiny of the Chinese maps* would show that since the thirties (even earlier) these showed the Karakorams as the border in the north of Kashmir, and this was not (seriously) challenged by the Government of India till 1958 in an *acute form*.

During 1946-1949, the period of the Republic of China headed by General Chiang-Kai-shek, the issue of the Northern border was not publicly raised by any side. But during the Asian Relations Conference in New Delhi in April, 1947, the Chinese delegates strongly protested against the display of a map of Asia, showing Tibet outside the boundaries of China, and consequently the map was withdrawn. There were, however, several official Notes exchanged bearing on the border issue during this period. On 16 October, 1947, the Government of Tibet sent a cable to the Government of India asking for the return of what were described as Tibetan territories from Assam to Ladakh, including such areas as Sikkim, Darjeeling and Bhutan. The Government of the Republic of China addressed four protest Notes to the British Embassy in China on the gradual encroachment by the British into Chinese-claimed territory south of the 'so-called McMahon Line' (July, September and November of 1946 and January 1947). The K.M.T. Government protested on the same issue by note with the Indian Embassy in China in February, 1947. On November 18, 1949, the Chinese Ambassador to India of the Nationalist Government delivered a Note to the Indian Ministry of External Affairs repudiating the Simla Convention which the Indian Government held to be valid. Since these Notes were kept confidential, the Indian public were unaware that they inherited from the British a vexing border problem in the North-East Frontier.

---

* e.g. The map attached to *The China Handbook (1937-43)* compiled by the China Ministry of Foreign Affairs . (New York : Macmillan Company.)

Soon after the recognition of the People's Government of China on 30 December 1949, the Government of India felt it necessary to make it clear to the public that they considered the McMahon Line as the legally valid boundary. In reply to a question by H. V. Kamath in Parliament on the international status of Tibet on 8th February, 1950, Nehru said, "In the early years of this century, a Convention was held between the representatives of then Government of India and Tibet and of China and at this certain decisions were arrived at. Roughly speaking, the decisions were about the boundary of Tibet and India called the McMahon Line, that Tibet should be treated as an autonomous country, and subject to China agreeing to this, some kind of Chinese sovereignty should be acknowledged. This was agreed to by them. But later, the then Government of China did not accept this agreement and therefore, did not sign it. In fact, although this agreement has been acted upon in India and Tibet, there has been no formal signature to it by the Chinese Government. So the matter stands there. Tibet is treated as an autonomous country and its exact relationship to China was not accepted by China."

On 17 March 1950, Debkanta Barooah revealed in Parliament facts which showed that Tibetan officials were forcibly collecting money from the NEFA hill tribes, and also that the Assam Government was making an annual payment of Rs. 5,000 to the Tawang Monastery in NEFA which was under Tibetan administration, and that the bulk of this money was sent to the Drepung monastery in Lhasa. So it came to be known that the Tibetans did not abide by the Simla Agreement of 1914, and still continued to occupy the Tawang area east of Bhutan.

A dangerous situation suddenly arose in the Far East with the outbreak of war in Korea on 25 June 1950. In the beginning, India thought North Korea to be responsible for launching an aggression against South Korea and supported the U.S. sponsored resolution in the U.N. Security Council recommending punitive measures against North Korea, a satellite of the Soviet Union. This resolution was passed in the absence of two great Powers, viz., the Soviet Union and the People's Republic of China. (Due to the U.S.A.'s opposition, the People's Republic of China could not take her seat as a permanent member of the Security Council and the Taiwan Government was allowed to represent

China. The Soviet Union boycotted the proceedings of the Security Council as a protest on this issue during the period from 13 January to 31 July 1950). There was resentment in China and the Soviet Union against India's siding with the West on a Cold War issue. Sardar K. M. Panikkar, the then Indian Ambassador to China, was able to provide a better appraisal of the facts about the Korean conflict and convince Nehru that there could be no settlement of the Korean conflict without bringing its next-door neighbours—the Soviet Union and the People's Republic of China—in the fold of the Security Council. On 13 July 1950, Nehru sent personal messages to Stalin and Acheson pleading for an early mediation to stop bloodshed in Korea, and stressed therein the necessity of the presence of the Soviet Union and the People's Republic of China in the Security Council. Though this peace overture was a failure due to American intransigence, it created a favourable atmosphere in India's starting a dialogue with China to tackle the bilateral issues such as Tibet.

In August 1950, there were several communications between the Indian Ambassador Sardar K. M. Panikkar and the Chinese Prime Minister Chou En-lai and the officials of the Chinese Foreign Ministry. In the Chinese Press and the radio at that time, there were constant allusions to the immediate necessity of 'liberating' Taiwan and Tibet. In an Indian Note dated 12 August 1950, it was stated that "the Government of India never had nor do they have now any political or territorial ambitions in Tibet." In this note, the Government of India also represented to the Government of China that they were concerned at the possibility of unsettled conditions across their border and strongly urged that the Sino-Tibetan relations should be stabilised through peaceful negotiations. The Chinese reply, dated 21 August 1950, stated that the Chinese Government was "happy to hear the desire of the Government of India to stabilise the Chinese-Indian border". It also expressed their willingness to solve the problem of Tibet by peaceful and friendly measures. On 22 August, Chou En-lai called Sardar Panikkar for a general discussion. In this conversation, Panikkar took the opportunity of pressing home the desirability of restraint and moderation in regard to Taiwan, and also raised the question of Tibet. Panikkar wrote in his memoirs : "In regard to Tibet, I knew they were a little uncertain about our attitude. I expressed the hope that they would follow a policy of peace in regard to Tibet. Chou En-lai replied that while the liberation of Tibet was a "sacred duty", his Government were anxious to secure their ends by negotiations and not by military action . . . . ".(*In Two Chinas* : p. 105). On 26 August, K. M. Panikkar in an *aide memoire* to the Chinese Government recognised the fact that the regional autonomy granted to Tibet was 'an autonomy within the confines of Chinese *sovereignty*' and added : "The recognised boundary between India and Tibet should remain inviolate". On 31st August 1950, the Chinese Ministry of Foreign Affairs informed the Indian Government through Ambassador Panikkar that the Chinese People's Liberation Army was going to take action soon in Western Sikang according to set plans and expressed the hope that the Indian Government would assist the delegation of the local authorities of Tibet so that it might arrive in Peking in mid-September to begin peace negotiations.

On 7 October 1950, when the U.N. Army under American Command decided to cross the 38th Parallel and invade North Korea, Nehru strongly opposed the action. Apart from the moral ground, Nehru was convinced that the invasion of North Korea was bound to result in the Chinese intervention and this might lead to an extension of the conflict in the Far East. The Chinese Army at this time launched an attack on Chamdo, a border town in the disputed area of Western Sikang. Chamdo fell on 19 October and the Chinese were poised for an invasion of Tibet. The Tibetan delegates called to Peking for negotiations for a political settlement had been nonchalantly procrastinating in India for more than six months on specious pleas, and apparently they received support from some high officials of the Indian External Affairs Ministry. On 25 October 1950, the Peking Radio broadcast that the process of liberating Tibet had begun. On 26 October, the Government of India sent a note to the Chinese Government protesting against the use of force in Tibet. On October 30, the Tibetan Government asked New Delhi for diplomatic assistance in the dispute with China. In their second Note dated 31 October 1950, India again made strong protests to China on the issue of sending an army into Tibet, and made it an occasion to remind China of certain privileges in Tibet which the Government of India had inherited from the British

Raj. (These related to the presence of an Indian Agent in Lhasa, existence of Trade Agencies at Gyantse and Yatung, maintenance of post and telegraph offices along the trade route up to Gyantse, and the existence of a small military escort at Gyantse). The Indian Note did not mention that these privileges arose mainly out of the secret Anglo-Tibetan Trade Regulations of 3 July 1914, an off-shoot of the Simla Convention of the same date declared illegal by the Republic of China. Though the Chinese Government resented this diplomatic interference by India in the matter of Tibet, the Chinese Army made no further movement westward from Chamdo. On the other hand, the Government of India did not try for long to dissuade the Tibetan delegation, till then staying in India, from going to Peking as they had implicitly warned in their Note to China dated 26th October, 1950.

But in October-November 1950, there were sharp differences within the Indian Government as to how much support should be given to the Tibetan Government in maintaining 'de facto' independence, which it had enjoyed since 1912. The Deputy Prime Minister Sardar Ballavbhai Patel was in favour of military intervention in Tibet and he had support from some members of the Cabinet, and the Foreign Office. But the Army Chief General Cariappa poured cold water into the plan of military intervention in Tibet to save it from China. (B. N. Mullik: *The Chinese Betrayal* pp. 80-81). The Tibetan Government was encouraged by some official groups in India to submit a complaint of invasion and aggression against Communist China on 7 November 1950, to the United Nations. When the matter was raised in the General Committee on 15 November 1950, it was decided that the Tibetan question should not be included in the General Assembly agenda. The Indian delegate in the Committee said that he was certain that a peaceful settlement could be reached and Tibet's autonomy could be safeguarded, and that the best way to ensure this was to abandon the idea of discussing the matter in the General Assembly. Failing to receive any sort of military or diplomatic support from the major powers, the Dalai Lama left Lhasa on 21 December 1950 to escape from the Chinese attack and settled at Yatung near the Indian border. The Dalai Lama also wrote to the Government of India seeking political asylum, but this was refused on the advice of K. M. Panikkar.

On 7 November 1950, Sardar Patel, who was in favour of an interventionist policy vis-a-vis Tibet, gave vent to his feelings in a confidential letter to Nehru. Sardar Patel asserted in this letter, ".... *The undefined state of frontier* and the existence on our side of a population with its affinities to Tibetans or Chinese have all the elements of potential trouble between China and ourselves.... Communism is no shield against imperialism and.... Communists are as good or as bad imperialists as any other. Chinese ambitions in this respect not only cover the Himalayan slopes on our side but also important parts of Assam." (Quoted in Kuldip Nayar's *Between the Lines*, p. 218). On 9 November 1950, Sardar Patel blurted out in a public speech that there might have been a world war in the issue of Tibet. In the context of a sharp division within the Cabinet, Nehru thought it necessary to assure the members of the Indian Parliament that "Map or no map. The McMahon Line is our definitive frontier, and no one will be allowed to cross that frontier." Nehru also assured the M.P.'s in the same speech that "The frontier from Ladakh to Nepal is defined chiefly by long usage and custom." (20 November, 1950). In answer to a question by an M.P., whether this boundary was recognised by the existing Tibetan Government, Nehru admitted that parts of the Indo-Tibetan boundary had not been recognised. But he did not make it clear, which parts of the boundary had not been accepted by the Tibetan Government. On 6 December 1950, Nehru repeated in Parliament an earlier statement of 17 March 1950 that the Himalayas formed India's traditional Northern frontier and that since Nepal was on this side of the Himalayas, any threat to the security of Nepal would be considered threat to India's security.

In November 1950, the Indian Government decided to set up a Committee under the Chairmanship of Major-General Himmatsinghji, the Deputy Minister of Defence, with representatives of Defence, Communication, Home and External Affairs Ministries to study the problems created by the Chinese invasion of Tibet. The North and North Eastern Border Defence Committee was established in February 1951. (The report of the Committee was submitted to the Defence Ministry in early 1953. The major recommendations of the Committee were "the reorganisation and expansion of the Assam Rifles, the extension of the administration in the NEFA, development of intelligence network along the border, development of civil armed police, development of communications and check posts." Prime Minister on *Sino-Indian Relations*, Vol. I : *In Parliament* (p. 251). The Border Defence Committee must have also recommended a precise definition of the North and North-east border, which it proposed to defend.

Due to the dangers of expansion of the Korean war in November 1950, the question of the Indo-Tibetan border was, however, relegated to the background for some time to come. The Chinese Army halted its march after the fall of Chamdo in the eastern border of Tibet. Nehru had been highly critical of the decision of the U.N. army under American leadership to cross the 38th Parallel to invade North Korea in October 1950. The collapse of General MacArthur's offensive in late November 1950 by the massive counter-attack launched by the ill-equipped Chinese Army, and President Truman's talk about the possibility of dropping an Atom Bomb enhanced the danger of a World War. This also stimulated anti-Western feelings throughout Asia. Nehru became conscious by then about the shift in the world balance of power caused by the emergence of China as a formidable land Power, able to face the American challenge in Asia, as also the advantageous position gained by India in holding a middle-ground in the new power balance. Nehru and his advisers thought as Mrs V. L. Pandit put it, ". . . war is a greater threat to us than Communism in Asia." (*N.Y. Times*, January 1, 1951). In this context it became necessary for India to avoid bickerings with China on the issue of Tibet, so that she might play the role of an honest peace-broker between the warring parties. In a B.B.C. broadcast from London on 13 January 1951, Nehru said, "China, in her new-found strength, has acted sometimes in a manner which I deeply regret. But we have to remember the background of China, as of other Asian countries — the long period of struggle and frustration, the insolent treatment that they received from imperialistic powers and the latter's refusal to deal with them in terms of equality. It is neither right nor practical to ignore the feelings of hundreds of millions of people. It is no longer safe to do so."

In January 1951, the Chinese and the U.N. Army led by the Americans were locked in severe battle in Korea in the wake of the Chinese counter-offensive, while India was busy leading Arab-Asian nations in the United Nations seeking a formula for peace based on *status quo ante bellum*. On February 2, the Government of India chose to take over Tawang which, though south of the McMahon Line, continued to be an important centre of Tibetan administration. There was no protest by China to the Government of India on the issue of Indian occupation of Tawang, while the Tibetans staged a demonstration before the Indian Mission in Lhasa when the news reached there. The quiet acquiscence of Communist China on the issue of Tawang convinced the Government of India that it would be possible to establish Indian control over the whole of the NEFA area without any opposition from Peking. This was quite in contrast to the attitude of the Nationalist Government of China, who had sent several protest Notes on the question of Indian incursion in the NEFA area. The north-eastern frontier was the only vulnerable area through which an attack might be launched by China against India—at least, this has been the opinion of the Indian Army Headquarters since 1910, when General Chao Er-feng's army moved about the NEFA area in their march on to Lhasa. Since the mid thirties, it has been an aim of the Foreign and Political Department of the Government of India to push the North-east frontier from the foothills to the crest line of the Himalayas. But due to stiff opposition of the Tibetan Government, with whom the British Government wanted to maintain best of terms with a view to use them as a buffer state vis-a-vis China, the mighty British Raj failed to implement the so-called McMahon Line as the North-eastern boundary of India. The taking over of Tawang in the first week of February 1951 without any opposition from the Chinese was rightly regarded by the Government of India as indicating that the People's Republic of China was psychologically prepared to accept the McMahon Line as the de facto boundary. On 1 February 1951, India and Burma were the only non-Communist Powers, which opposed the U.S. sponsored resolution in the U.N. General Assembly declaring China as guilty of aggression in Korea. This led to a further improvement in Sino-Indian relations during this period. On 12 February 1951, Nehru told the Indian Parliament, "The House will remember that we were aggrieved at a certain turn of events in Tibet, but we did not allow that to affect our policy or our desire to maintain friendly relations with the People's Government of China. I am glad to say that our relations with the New China are friendly at present."

On 28 March 1951, B. V. Keskar, the Deputy Minister for External Affairs, explained India's policy in regard to the Indo-Tibetan frontier in the Indian Parliament : "The Government is not unmindful of the protection of our frontiers adjoining Tibet. I may go further and say that the Government feels that the best way of protecting that frontier is to have a friendly Tibet and a friendly China. It is obvious that such a complicated and big frontier cannot be well-protected if we have a border country which becomes hostile to us. Therefore, we feel that in tackling the question of Tibet and China, we should always keep in mind that a friendly China and a friendly Tibet are the best guarantee of the defence of our country." (*Parliamentary Debates,* Volume IX, 1951 *Third Session, Second Part* col. 5320).

By the end of 1950, the Tibetan Government had realised that neither India nor the Great Powers were prepared to give them diplomatic or military support to bolster up their pretensions of independence. In April 1951, negotiations started in Peking between the Chinese and Tibetan delegations and this resulted in a 14-point Agreement on 23 May 1951. This Agreement gave assurance of local autonomy, but provided for the gradual incorporation of the Tibetan Army into the People's Liberation Army of China, and the exclusive handling of the foreign affairs by the Central People's Government of China.

From a speech delivered by Nehru in Parliament on 25 November 1959, we get a chronology of Sino-Indian negotiations on the question of Tibet during 1951-1952. ". . . in an informal conversation with the Indian Ambassador on the 27th September 1951, Premier Chou En-lai expressed his anxiety to safeguard in every way Indian interests in Tibet on which matter 'there was no territorial dispute or controversy between India and China.' ." He added: "The question of stabilisation of the Tibetan frontier was a matter of common interest to India, Nepal and China and could best be done by discussions between the three countries. Since the Chinese Army entered Lhasa in pursuance of the Sino-Tibetan Agreement of 1951 to take up frontier posts, it was necessary to settle the matter as early as possible." . . . On 4 October 1951, the Indian Ambassador in Peking . . . informed the

Chinese Premier, that the Government of India would welcome negotiations on the subjects mentioned by Premier Chou En-lai".

Sardar Panikkar came to India in October 1951, and had consultations in the External Affairs Ministry about the attitude to be adopted regarding Tibet. "Panikkar hoped that the Chinese would not move a considerable armed force into Tibet... he further said that extra-territorial rights had no place in the relationship between two independent countries in modern times and India would put herself entirely in the wrong by insisting on the continuance of the rights which the British had forcibly extorted from Tibet. In any case China would not agree to their continuance and there was no way by which India could enforce them except by force of arms which India was not in a position to employ. So the best policy would be to give up gracefully all that was untenable and insist on economic and cultural rights which were of a more fundamental nature and were not necessarily based on treaties. Panikkar's views were shared by the Government of India." (B. N. Mullik : *My Years with Nehru*, p. 147).

In February 1952, the Indian Ambassador in a meeting with the Chinese Premier gave a statement of the existing Indian rights in Tibet and reiterated India's willingness to arrive at a mutually satisfactory settlement. Premier Chou En-lai replied that there was "no difficulty in safeguarding the economic and cultural interests of India in Tibet". He did not refer to the frontier question in his reply; nor did the Indian Ambassador raise this question specifically then. (*Nehru's speech in Parliament* on November 25, 1959).

In May 1952, before his departure from China, Panikkar had further conversations with Chou En-lai regarding Tibet. While accepting the legitimacy of our trade and cultural interests in that area, he suggested that the Political Agency in Lhasa, an office of dubious legality, should be regularised by its transformation into an Indian Consulate in exchange for a similar Chinese office in Bombay. So far as our other posts and institutions were concerned, some of them like telegraph lines, military escort at Yatung, were to be abolished quietly in time, and the trade agents and other subordinate agencies brought within the framework of our normal consulate relations. These were to be taken up when circumstances were ripe. In *Two Chinas*, p. 175). Neither side raised the issue of the boundary.

It has been brought to light by Neville Maxwell that in 1952, Sir G. S. Bajpai, the first Secretary-General of the External Affairs Ministry, who retired in May and was posted as the Governor of the Bombay province, wrote a letter to his old Ministry, urging that India should take the initiative in raising the question of the McMahon Line with the Chinese Government. He warned that to China the McMahon line might be one of those 'scars left by Britain in the course of her aggression against China, who may seek to heal or erase this scar on the basis of frontier rectifications that may not be either to our liking or our interest.'

Nehru discussed this suggestion with K. M. Panikkar, the Ambassador to China, who was in New Delhi for consultations, and Panikkar replied to Bajpai. He told him that the Prime Minister had decided that it was not in India's interest to raise the question of the McMahon Line. Nehru, he explained, had taken the view that since India had unequivocally and publicly stated that she regarded the McMahon Line as the boundary, it should be left to China to raise the subject. If India were to do so, "we should force the Chinese to one of two attitudes: either the acceptance of a treaty signed by us with Tibet, or a refusal of it coupled with an offer to negotiate. The first is not altogether easy to imagine, considering that every previous Chinese Government has refused in terms to accept an Indo-Tibetan treaty as binding on them. The second would not be advantageous to us."

"If, on the other hand, 'China raised the issue', Panikkar went on, 'we can plainly refuse to reopen the question and take our stand that the Prime Minister took it in his public statement, that the territory on this side of the McMahon Line is ours, and there is nothing to discuss about it."

After the departure of Sardar Panikkar from Peking, there were some bickerings between the Governments of India and China in July-August 1952 over the despatch of fresh Indian troops to replace the guards at Gyantse and Yatung, the seizure of the wireless set of the Indian Trade Agent at Gartok, refusal to allow the Political Officer in Sikkim to visit Lhasa without a proper Chinese visa. (B. N. Mullik : *My Years with Nehru* pp. 149-150). But again, the issue of the Indo-Tibetan border was not raised by any side. On 15 September 1952 there was an official announcement in New Delhi that the Indian Mission in Lhasa was henceforth to be designated as Consulate-General, and that three Trade Agencies at Gyantse, Gartok and Yatung were to be under the general supervision of the Consulate in Lhasa. In the press *communique'* it was declared that the change in status resulted from the fact that the foreign relations of Tibet were currently conducted by the People's Republic of China.

Since October 1952, India's diplomatic activities were concentrated in bringing the Korean War to a close through devising a compromise formula on the vexed question of the repatriation of the prisoners of war. The question of P.O.W.s hamstrung the armistice negotiations for about two years. The coming to power of the Republican Party in the U.S.A. meant that the influence of the China Lobby, who were pledged to 'roll back the mud tide of Communism in Asia', was ascendent in American politics. The armistice in Korea was signed in July 1953, mainly on the basis of an Indian formula, but India was excluded from the membership of the proposed political conference on Korea in the voting of the U.N. General Assembly due to the hostile attitude of the U.S.A. towards Indian neutralism. India had also become aware of the negotiations going on between the U.S.A. and Pakistan about bringing Pakistan into a Military Alliance with the U.S.A. as early as September 1952. The aggravation of the conflict in Indo-China in 1953 also contained new portents of a widespread conflict in Asia. In this context of a danger of war in Asia due to threat of American expansionism prompted the Government of India to mend their fences with China. In September 1953, the Government of India approached the People's Government of China for negotiations regarding the outstanding questions concerning Tibet.

In November 1953 there were further discussions in the External Affairs Ministry in New Delhi, in which it was again decided that the question of the Indo-Tibetan boundary was not to be raised in the forthcoming conference with China in Peking. According to B. N. Mullik, "...one view expressed during the briefing of our delegation was that the question of India's northern frontier should also be settled during the negotiations. But the general view was that we should not allow China to take this opportunity to rake up the whole issue. In any case, China was not going to recognise the McMahon line which we considered to be our northern frontier and so there could not be any negotiations on that score." (*My Years With Nehru* : pp. 155-156).

The Conference opened in Peking on 31 December 1953. Premier Chou En-lai at the first meeting said that the relations between China and India were becoming closer every day and that from among the outstanding questions the two sides could settle questions which were ripe for settlement. The Indian Ambassador then pointed out that there were only small questions pending between India and China, but he wished to see nothing big or small remaining outstanding between the two countries. Premier Chou En-lai replied that two large countries like India and China with a long common frontier were bound to have some questions, but all questions could be settled smoothly. (See *Note of the Government of India to the Chinese Government*, 12 February 1960 : *White Paper No. III*, p. 91). According to B. N. Mullik, "....the conference started with the two sides speaking in two voices, the Indians insisting that all "pending questions" should be discussed and settled and the Chinese holding the view that only "such questions as were ripe for discussion" should be taken up leaving the rest for future settlement. In India's view the border question did not exist but the Chinese kept this issue open to be taken up when a suitable occasion would arise." (*My Years with Nehru* : p. 151).

The Agreement "on Trade and Intercourse between Tibet Region of China and India" was signed on 29 April 1954. India gave up all the extra-territorial rights which the British Government in India had exercised in Tibet by virtue of the secret Anglo-Tibetan Trade Regulations of July 1914. The central provisions of the Agreement dealt with the regulation of trade markets, routes and procedures for traders and pilgrims. The treaty provisions were supplemented by a Note dealing with the withdrawal of Indian military escorts and the handing over of Indian post and telegraph facilities and the Indian rest-houses to the Chinese. The most important element of the treaty was contained in the title of the agreement itself in which Tibet was referred to as "Tibet region of China." This was a definite assurance to China that India had discarded once for all the British policy of bolstering up Tibet as a buffer state. The preamble to the Agreement contained the five principles (1) mutual respect for each other's territorial integrity and sovereignty, (2) mutual non-aggression, (3) mutual non-interference in each other's internal affairs, (4) equality and mutual benefit, and (5) peaceful co-existence. Of these (1) and (4) are the basic principles declared by Chairman Mao Tse-tung on 1 October, 1949 to be followed by the People's Republic of China in establishing diplomatic relations with foreign governments. The points (2) and (3) provided a sort of reassurance of China's peaceful intent towards India. Peaceful Co-existence was the common desire of both sides.

The boundary question arose only indirectly during discussions on Article 4. The Chinese side introduced a draft stating that the Chinese Government 'agrees to open a number of mountain passes.' The Indian side objected on the ground that this was a way of claiming ownership over what were in fact border passes. These Chinese then withdraw their draft by describing it as a concession. Finally it was laid down that pilgrims and traders could travel through the following passes and routes : (i) Shipki La; (ii) Mana Pass; (iii) Niti Pass; (iv) Kungri Bingri Pass; (v) Darma Pass; (vi) Lipu Lekh Pass.

It is curious to note that the border passes regulating the flow of trans-Himalayan trade and pilgrimage mentioned in the 1954 Agreement belonged to the Central sector of the border only. There was no reference to border passes either in the Eastern sector where a potential dispute in regard to the Indian claim to the McMahon Line existed, or in the Western sector which represented the frontier of the Kashmir state. The Government of India must have deliberately avoided raising the issue of border passes in the Eastern sector of the frontier and the Chinese also kept silent on the issue denoting tacit acceptance of the McMahon Line. But it is now known from the authoritative source of the Indian I. B. Chief that the Indian side did try to fix border marts in the Western Tibet for the benefit of Ladakhi traders. But, "... the Chinese delegate would not discuss the question of trade marts in Western Tibet on the ground that this related to Kashmir which was under dispute between India and Pakistan." (*My Years With Nehru*, p. 153). B. N. Mullik also refers to "the refusal of the Chinese to recognise the customary trade mart in Rudok (Western Tibet) without ascribing any particular reason," and comments, "This was no doubt because the Chinese were building the road from Rudok to Sinkiang via Aksai Chin." (Ibid p. 153).

Though both India and China were eager to reach an agreement in the context of the worsening international situation caused by the policy of 'Brinkmanship' declared by the American Secretary of State, there was tough bargaining when the Chinese delegates insisted on having a trade establishment in 'strategic' Simla. The Agreement was held up for six weeks over the proposal. Nehru succeeded in giving that right in Delhi, instead. "Finally Peking agreed on Delhi because it wanted the fact of the agreement to become known about the time the Geneva Conference opened." (INSAF in The Hindustan Times, 7 May 1954).

The Sino-Indian Agreement had mixed reception in the Indian Press. There was a hope that in return to handing over the privileges enjoyed in Tibet due to the British legacy, India might be permitted to reopen her consulate in Kashgar (Sinkiang). But the Kashgar consulate could not be included in the agenda in as much as the People's Republic of China had declared Sinkiang a 'Closed area'. It was admittedly a great gain that India could establish a Consulate in Lhasa, an ideal listening post for Central Asia on a regular basis. The Indian Mission established by the British in Lhasa in the thirties was an office of dubious legality.

According to S. S. Khera, former Cabinet Secretary and Principal Defence Secretary to the Government of India, "Nehru, with his sense of history and of the need for long-term stability of friendly relations between the two great and ancient nations, had hoped for a 25-year agreement in the first instance. But the Indian negotiators succeeded in achieving only a comparatively short-term agreement for 8 years . . . .

"Jawaharlal Nehru was disappointed. Also late in the day as it was, his suspicions about the Chinese intentions were aroused. He stoutly defended the 1954 Agreement; but he also gave instructions to set up border posts, to safeguard the country's northern frontiers." (*India's Defence Problem,* p. 155).

According to D. R. Mankekar, Nehru addressed a secret memorandum to the External Affairs Ministry, Defence Ministry and Home Ministry on the Sino-Indian border question in July 1954.

"In this memorandum Nehru described the Agreement as the new starting point of our relations with China and Tibet, and affirmed that both as flowing from our policy and as a consequence of our Agreement with China, the Northern frontier should be considered a firm and definite one, which was not open to discussion with any body. The Prime Minister directed that a system of check-posts should be spread along this entire frontier more specially in such places as might be considered disputed areas." (*The Guilty Men of* 1962, Page 138). Along with this memorandum was issued a new version of Survey of India maps showing the whole northern frontier as clearly defined replacing the old official maps (e.g. *The Political map of India* 1950 : Scale 1 inch = 70 miles), which showed the northern frontier extending from the north-west end of Kashmir to Nepal as 'undefined', and the McMahon line as 'undemarcated'.

II—1954-1959

Before July 1954, there were only a few trouble spots on India's northern frontier. We have already referred to the exchange of several notes between the Nationalist Government of China and the Government of India during the period from 1944 to 1949. These Notes arose due to the Government of India's efforts to push their check-posts in the North-east frontier region from the foot-hills of Assam towards the vicinity of the McMahon Line. But since the establishment of the People's Republic of China in October 1949, no issues were raised by the Government of China on the persistent efforts of the Government of India to bring the Tribal peoples under the control of the North-eastern Frontier Agency set up in 1950 under the Constitution of the Indian Republic. In the central sector, there was a recurrence of an old dispute in 1951 and 1953 in the Tehri-Garhwal region near Gum-gum Nallah. In 1926, a Boundary Commission consisting of the representatives of Tibet, Tehri-Garhwal and the Government of India met at Nilang, but no agreement could be reached since then. There were no disputes in the Kashmir sector, though one of the Chinese armies which marched into Tibet in the fall of 1950 travelled by the Aksai Chin route from Sinkiang to Western Tibet. This is corroborated by Hugh Richardson in his book : *Tibet and Its History* p. 229. "A report on the presence of the Chinese troops in West Tibet and their advance from Sinkiang province was contained in an official despatch from the Government of India's Agent at Gartok, Mr. Garpon Marlampa." (*The Statesman,* 15 November 1950). According to S. S. Khera, "Information about the activities of the Chinese on the Indo-Tibetan border, particularly on the Aksai Chin region, had begun to come in by about 1952 or even earlier. Subsequent events have shown that much of this activity was connected with the opening up of the road through the Aksai Chin region of Ladakh, and along the South Tibetan border towards Central Tibet and Lhasa ... However, no great significance appears to have been attached to the earliest reports of these movements from China into Western Tibet. But by about 1952 and in any case well before the 1954 Agreement, the developments had become too obvious to be ignored. (*India's Defence problem,* p. 157). Until June 1954, the current Survey of India maps showed the northern as well as the eastern boundary of Kashmir as undefined. Also the future of Kashmir was still uncertain, India being committed to the verdict of an internationally supervised plebiscite, subject to the prior withdrawal of Pakistani armed personnel from its territory. These seem to be the real reasons why the Government of India kept silent for several years, even though they knew about the Chinese presence in the Aksai Chin region. Also they knew that the Head Lama of Ladakh, Kushuk-Bakola warned in June 1952, that Ladakh might seek political union with Tibet "as a last course left to us." (Vide *The Danger In Kashmir* : Josef Korbel (Revised edition), pp. 230, 231 and 233).

From the study of the White Papers published by the Government of India, we find that since July 1954 to July 1958, the protest Notes of the Governments of China and India were concerned with small areas of dispute such as Barahoti, Damzan (both south of the Niti Pass), the Nilang area in Tehri-Garhwal, the Shipki Pass in the central sector. These disputes arose just after the signing of the Panch Sheel Agreement over Tibet due to several reasons. In the Central sector, the Indo-Tibetan Border Force under the Home Ministry set up new check-posts in the previously disputed areas in accordance with the secret memorandum issued by Nehru in July 1954. The Chinese, on the other hand, were taking up a survey of the border region in this sector for the first time, and as the new overlords of Tibet, they were prone to support Tibetan irredentist claims in respect of the boundary. But these disputes did not form a part of the conversations between Nehru and Chou En-lai during the visits of the Chinese Premier to India in the winter of 1956-1957. They talked only about the North-eastern section of the Indian frontier. Nehru had discussed the Burma border in a recent letter to Chou En-lai in 1956, presumably because he thought that a satisfactory solution of the Burma's northern border on the basis of the McMahon Line would strengthen India's position about the remaining section of the Line. Nehru got the impression that while Chou En-lai did not approve of this border being called the McMahon line, he had accepted the McMahon Line border with Burma, and whatever might have happened long ago he proposed to accept this border with India also, after due consultation with the authorities of the Tibet region "in consideration of the friendly relations between India and China." Nehru did not raise the issue of the Kashmir border. (At a Press conference in Calcutta on 9 December 1956, Prime Minister Chou En-lai characterised the Kashmir question as 'an outstanding issue between India and Pakistan.')

On 21 August, 1958, the Government of India sent a protest Note to the Counsellor of China in India on the publication of a map of China in *The China Pictorial* (July 1958) on the ground of inaccuracies in the delineation of the Sino-Indian borders. In this Note, for the first time objection was taken by the Government of India about large areas of Ladakh, eastern part of the Kashmir territory—disputed between India and Pakistan—being shown as Chinese territory. Before this, there was another minor dispute in regard to the Ladakh region of Kashmir. On 2 July 1958, a *Note Verbale* was handed by the Ministry of External Affairs to the Chinese Counsellor in India about the occupation of Khurnak fort in Eastern Ladakh by the Chinese troops. On 18 October 1958, the Foreign Secretary of the Government of India handed over to the Chinese Ambassador an informal Note protesting that the Chinese had constructed a part of the Yehcheng-Gartok road "through indisputably Indian territory without first obtaining the permission of the Government of India and without even informing the Government of India." This letter also made an enquiry about an Army patrol of 15 people and 34 ponies which were out "on normal patrol" in this area and did not return. The Foreign Secretary referred to these incidents as "petty frontier disputes." On 8 November 1958, the Note submitted by the Indian Ambassador to the Chinese Vice-Minister for Foreign Affairs said *inter alia*, "It is now clear that the Chinese also claim this area as their territory. The question whether a particular area is Indian or Chinese territory is a matter in dispute which has to be dealt separately." But Prime Minister Nehru's letter to Premier Chou En-lai, dated 14 December 1958, which mainly dealt with the border between India and China did not make any reference to the Ladakh i.e. Kashmir section of the frontier. This seems to imply that the letter of the Foreign Secretary, dated 18 October 1958, was issued mainly to secure the information and release of the Army personnel, who had been sent to explore the exact location of the Sinkiang-Tibet highway and had been arrested by the Chinese at Haji Langar in the summer of 1958.

According to the I. B. Chief B. N. Mullik, ".... enough information was available about the construction of the road right from 1951 to 1957, when the road was formally declared open ... All through these years no questions were raised by the Army Headquarters or the Ministry of External Affairs about this road. It was only after the road had been completed and heavy traffic had started plying that some attention was turned on it though even then, ... it was only considered to be of nuisance value and not one that affected our security. (*My years with Nehru,* p. 199).

The first Director of the Historical Division, Ministry of External Affairs, Professor K. Zachariah informed the North and North-East Border Committee (1951-53), that during the days of the British Raj, the Government of India maps showed consistently a definite alignment only in the North-West corner of Kashmir viz. the Gilgit region facing the border of the Russian Empire just beyond the narrow strip of Afghan territory known as the Wakhan corridor. There were in the main three conceptions of the North and North-Eastern boundary of Kashmir put forward by British officials and cartographers, and explorers at different times :

1. There was the John Ardagh Line showing a boundary alignment which took the crest of the Kuenlun range and enclosed within the British territory the upper reaches of the Yarkand river and its tributaries and the Karakash river as well as the whole of the Aksai Chin plateau. (This was a strategic adaptation of the Johnson boundary of 1865).

2. There was the Macartney-Macdonald line (1899), which put forth a less ambitious claim of territory north of the Karakoram range. East of the Karakoram Pass, it left to China the whole of the Karakash Valley and almost all of Aksai Chin proper. It followed the Lak Tsang range which left on the Indian side, the Lingzi Tang salt plains and the whole of the Chang Chenmo valley, as well as the Chip Chap river further north.

3. Then there was the Karakoram Line, which was based on the watershed principle [The Map of India attached to the *Report of The Indian Statutory Commission*, Volume I (1930), shows the Karakoram alignment depicting the North and Northeast boundary of Kashmir].

Scanning the Survey of India maps during the last decade before independence, we find the Map of India (showing Provinces, States & Districts: Scale 1 Inch to 70 Miles) published in 1938, failed to show any boundary line or colour difference along the wide region between Kashmir and Sinkiang/Tibet. Since 1945, however, though the North and the Eastern boundary of Kashmir were shown as 'Undefined', an attempt was made by means of a colour-wash to convey a vague idea of the North and Eastern boundaries of Kashmir, more or less in conformity with the Ardagh line in the region, east of the Karakoram Pass. (This change was made apparently on the initiative of Sir Olaf Caroe, who was then the Foreign Secretary to the Government of India. This practice was followed by the Government of free India in regard to Maps showing the North and Eastern boundaries of Kashmir, which were current till June 1954).

In the new map of India issued in July 1954, the words 'Boundary Undefined' were erased, and by this simple process the Survey of India maps laid claim to a boundary alignment of Kashmir east of the Karakoram Pass akin to the John Ardagh Line, including the whole of Aksai Chin and reaching the Kuenlun Mountain in the north-east. Though in his circular of July 1954 to the Ministries of External Affairs, Home and Defence, Nehru ruled that "the northern border should be considered a firm and definite one which was not open to discussion with anybody", no action was taken to push the check-posts to the forward areas in the Kashmir sector, as was done in the middle and eastern sections of the Northern boundary. Regarding the setting up up checkposts in the Aksai Chin region, "The Army's attitude was that they could send an occasional patrol but they were in no position to open and hold any posts in this area . . . it would be difficult to oust the Chinese from this region. In any case, the army was in no position to make that effort because of the limited resources available at Leh and of the non-existence of any road communication from Leh to these parts." (B. N. Mullik : *My years with Nehru,* p. 201).

It appears that the Government of India's unilateral decision in July to issue new maps of India with a well-defined Northern boundary, incorporating a version of the John Ardagh Line in the Kashmir sector east of the Karakoram Pass, was primarily meant to provide a bargaining counter in boundary negotiations with China, which were inevitable at some future date. It is significant that even in August-September 1959, when Nehru had to face an angry Parliament in the context of the concurrent leakage about the border clash at Longju and the construction of the Chinese highway through Aksai Chin, Nehru maintained a pliant attitude about the exact location of the frontier in the Ladakh region while asserting a firm claim about the McMahon Line all along. On 28 August 1959, Nehru said, "This was the boundary of the old Kashmir state with Tibet and Chinese Turkestan. Nobody had marked it . . . But after some kind of broad surveys, the then Government had laid down that border which we have been accepting . . . the Aksai Chin area is an area about some parts of which . . . it is not quite clear what the position is." On 31 August 1959, Nehru said, "The position in Ladakh is different from the position in the North Eastern Frontier Agency . . . . the Ladakh border was for these long years under the Jammu & Kashmir State and nobody knew exactly what was happening there, although some British officers went a hundred years ago and drew a line and the Chinese did not accept that line. The matter is clearly one for consideration and debate. . . ."

Nehru spoke in the same vein about the border of Ladakh in Parliament on September 10 and September 12.

Neville Maxwell quoted a official directive issued by Nehru on 13 September 1959, which also reveals his desire for a compromise settlement in the Ladakh sector of the boundary: "... (d) The Aksai Chin area has to be left more or less as it is, as we have no check-posts there and practically little of access. Any questions in relation to it can only be considered when the time arises, in the context of the larger question of the entire border. For the present, we have to put up with the Chinese occupation of this north-eastern sector (of Ladakh) and their road across it ...." (*India's China War,* p. 130).

In the original resolution of the Working Committee of the Congress Party, drafted on 25 September 1959, for the A.I.C.C. session held in Chandigarh (25-28 September), there was a reference to "the recent developments on the *North-East frontier of India*" only, there being no specific reference to the Ladakh region. This was objected to by many members of the A.I.C.C. and the resolution was suitably amended. From this report published in The Hindu, 28 September 1959, we can presume that the Congress High Command also was not sure about the Indian claim on Aksai Chin.

In spite of Nehru's directive of 13 September prohibiting further movement in the Ladakh region, the Indo-Tibetan border force under the Home Ministry was involved in a clash with the Chinese border force near the Kongka Pass on 21 October 1959, in which 9 Indian policemen lost their lives. This incident marked a critical point in the Sino-Indian frontier dispute, which hamstrung Indian diplomacy by rousing public anger to a boiling point. On 23 October 1959, the Ministry of External Affairs submitted a Note to the Chinese Ambassador in New Delhi protesting against the "sudden and aggressive firing by Chinese forces in the region of the Kongka Pass" and "intrusion by Chinese troops into an area which is part of Indian territory." This Note claimed that this area was about 40 to 50 miles west of the traditional Sino-Indian frontier which has been shown in official Indian maps. However, from the testimony of Karam Singh, the Commander of the Indo-Tibetan Border force which clashed with the Chinese patrols near the Kongka Pass, it would appear that one Sharma, Deputy Director in the Ministry of Home

Affairs, gave him instruction to establish new check-posts in forward areas in Ladakh on 22 September 1959. (Vide *White Paper III* p. 14). This shows that some officials of the Home Ministry and its underlings—such as the Indo-Tibetan border force as well as the Intelligence Bureau—were nonchalantly flouting the directive of Nehru dated 13 September 1959, prohibiting forward movement of patrols in the Ladakh sector, and that led to the critical Kongka Pass incident of 21 October 1959. B. N. Mullik writes, "On October 23, when the facts of the outrage came to be known, the Prime Minister held a meeting which was attended by the Defence Minister, the Chief of the Army Staff and officers from the Ministries of External Affairs, Home and Defence... The Intelligence Bureau was made the common target by the Army Headquarters and the External Affairs Ministry and accused of expansionism and causing provocations on the frontier ... The Army demanded that no further movements of armed police should take place on the frontier without their clearance... the Prime Minister had to give in to the Army's demand. The result was that the protection of the border was thereafter handed over to the Army and all operations of armed police were made subject to prior approval of the Army command..." (*My Years With Nehru,* pp. 243-44). Thus we have B. N. Mullik's own testimony to show that while the Government of India publicly accused China of 'unprovoked aggression' at the Kongka Pass, within the inner conclave of the Government the blame for provocation and *'aggression'* was squarely laid on the Intelligence Bureau.

It was since November 1959 that Nehru took a rigid attitude about India's border claims in the Kashmir sector. The Note of the Ministry of External Affairs to the Embassy of China dated 4 November 1959 described in details for the first time the boundary claimed by the Government, specially in the section eastward from the Karakoram Pass. "From the Karakoram Pass this boundary proceeds north-east via Qara Tagh Pass and then follows the Kuenlun range from a point 15 miles north of Haji Langer to Peak 21250 (Survey of India Map) which lies east of Longitude 80 east." This Note also made a strange assertion that "This line constitutes the watershed between the Indus system in India and the Khotan system in China", while according to authoritative opinion, the Karakoram Mountains—which extend south-east of the Karakoram Pass—form the watershed between the Indus system and the Khotan system. The famous Swedish explorer Dr Sven Hedin, Professor Owen Lattimore, *The Imperial Gazeteer* Vol. XV (1908), *The Chambers Gazeteer* (1962), *The Columbia Encyclopedia* (1963)—all agree that the Karakoram Mountains are the main water-divide in this region. In early November 1959, the Historical Division of the External Affairs Ministry produced a Note on *The Historical Background of the Himalayan Frontier of India.* It was asserted therein, "India's northern frontier has lain where it now runs for nearly three thousand years. The areas along this frontier, which is nearly 2,500 miles long from the Kuenlun Mountains in the far north to the junction with Burma in the east, have always been a part of India." This Note also asserted the sacrosant nature of the northern frontier saying, "This northern frontier of India is for much of its length the crest of the Himalayan ranges. The Himalayas have always dominated Indian life, just as they have dominated the Indian landscape." The well-known Indian columnist *'Waqnis'* rightly condemned this document for 'wrong statement of facts and illogical references' and said, ".....I do wish that this essay into history assisted by cruches of impressive statement had not been made." (*The Statesman*, 23 November 1959). This document, however, served to add fuel to the fire of nationalist passions and prejudices in the context of the Kongka Pass incidents, as the true nature and origin of the conflict remained unrevealed to the Indian public. In early November 1959, Nehru sent a secret memorandum to key Ambassadors abroad which said *inter alia* : "He is convinced now that China in the present dispute is only after territorial gains from India and not interested in a settlement based on *traditional frontiers* : therefore he does not see much chance of a reasonable negotiated settlement of the dispute." (*The Hindu*, 13 November 1959). According to Neville Maxwell, this sea-change in Nehru's thinking about India's traditional claim to India's frontiers was very much influenced by Dr S. Gopal, Director, Historical Division, External Affairs Ministry, who had been sent to London to go through the material on India's borders in the India Office and Foreign Office archives and make an objective appraisal of historical evidence. "In November 1959 Gopal told Nehru that India's claim to the

Aksai Chin area was clearly stronger than China's". (*India's China War*, p. 119). What sort of historical evidence, Dr Gopal dug up in London, which would establish Indian claims over the Aksai Chin area, still remains a mystery. No such document is available in the archives of the India Office Library and Records.

The Historical Division of the External Affairs Ministry must also be held responsible for Nehru's misquoting of the 1899 boundary proposals which the British Minister in Peking, Sir Claude Macdonald, made to the Tsungli Yamen (Chinese Foreign Office). In his letter to Prime Minister Chou En-Lai, Nehru said *inter alia* "The proposal made by the British Government referred not to the Eastern Frontier of Ladakh with Tibet but to the Northern Frontier of Ladakh and Kashmir with Sinkiang. It was stated in that context that *the northern boundary ran along the Kuenlun range to a point of 80° east longitude,* where it met the eastern boundary of Ladakh". The relevant portion of the actual document of 1899 says, that the proposed boundary is to follow "the Lak Tsung Range until that *meets the spur running south from the K'un-lun range,* which has been shown in our maps as the eastern boundary of Ladakh. This is a little east of 80° east longitude." (Quoted by Alastair Lamb : *The China-India Border,* p. 182). This is another example to show how Nehru was ill-served by the Historical Division of the External Affairs Ministry in tackling the Sino-Indian frontier dispute on a rational basis. (By the textual alteration, the Macartney-Macdonald line was misrepresented to include the whole of the Aksai Chin area within the Indian boundary).

III
CONCLUDING REMARKS

From the statements of Nehru in Parliament at well as his letters to Premier Chou-En-lai in 1958-1959, it appears that regarding the claim to the McMahon Line, he was completely relying on the information given in the official publication of the British Government of India viz. *Collection of Engagements, Treaties and Sanads* published under the authority of the Foreign and Political Department : Volume XIV, more widely known by the name of its first editor as *Aitchison's Treaties* relating to

Tibet. This volume, carrying the date of imprint 1929, was supposed to have given the official version of the results of the Tripartite Simla Conference held between Britain, China and Tibet in 1913-14. This publication convinced Nehru, Krishna Menon, Sir G. S. Bajpai, S. Dutt, who served as Foreign Secretary during 1954-1961, as also most other key officials in the External Affairs Ministry that the Simla Convention of July 1914 was concerned with the fixation of both the Sino-Tibetan border and the Indo-Tibetan border. After initialling the agreement, the Chinese delegate failed to put in his full signature and withdrew from the Conference by way of dissent after lodging a protest in respect to the Sino-Tibetan boundary. Since the Chinese did not raise an issue in regard to the Indo-Tibetan boundary fixed along the main axis of the Himalayas, and since India and Tibet ratified the Simla Convention by means of a declaration accepting its terms as binding as between themselves, the Indo-Tibetan boundary (later known as the McMahon Line) should be regarded as being legally valid since July 1914.

Recent researches in the records of the India Office, London have revealed that the Simla Conference (1913-1914) was concerned with the fixation of only the Sino-Tibetan boundary. Sir Henry McMahon's Memorandum with regard to the North-east frontier of India did not carry the endorsement of the then Government of India. The Government of India regarded the Simla Convention as abortive due to the Chinese refusal to ratify the agreement. Due to the prohibitory clauses of the Anglo-Russian Convention (1907), the Government of India was legally debarred from signing a bilateral agreement with Tibet, which was under the suzerainty of China. Recent researches in the records of the India Office, London also reveal that the volume (XIV) of the *Aitchison's Treaties* relating to Tibet on which the Government of India was relying for authentic information in regard to the Simla Convention was a spurious document published in 1938 with the imprint of 1929, while the original version was withdrawn from circulation. The issue of the spurious version of the *Aitchison's Treaties* relating to Tibet in 1938 asserting the McMahon Line as a legally valid boundary also coincided with the issue of new maps by the Survey of India for the first time showing the North-eastern boundary along the main Himalayan axis cancelling the old maps, which showed the Assam boundary along the foothills of the Himalayas. These devices were adopted by the Department of External Affairs, New Delhi mainly on the initiative of Sir Olaf Caroe, then a Deputy Secretary. Their main purpose was to reopen the issue of the North-eastern boundary with the Tibetan Government, who had ignored the secret boundary agreement with the British all these years with impunity and showed reluctance to accept its validity without a *quid pro quo* in the fulfilment of Tibetan boundary claims vis-a-vis China. But Sir Olaf Caroe's persistent efforts to make the Tibetan Government agree to the McMahon Line proved to be infructuous as is revealed in the reports of the British emissaries to Lhasa (Sir Basil Gould, Rai Bahadur Norbu, and A. J. Hopkinson), available in the India Office records. Thus, free India was left with a difficult legacy in regard to the North-east frontier. In 1943, the Government of India made an indirect effort to endow the Simla Convention with *ex post facto* legality by trying to secure American recognition of Tibet's *de facto* independence beneath "formal Chinese suzerainty". They specifically urged the U.S.A. to recognise Tibet's right "to exchange diplomatic representatives with other powers." But the U.S.A. rejected the proposal on the ground that they regarded Tibet among the areas constituting the Republic of China. [See author's article on The McMahon Line, *1914-1915* in The China Quarterly, July-September 1971].

From the geographic point of view, however, the McMahon Line may be regarded as a natural border between India and China, as it represents approximately the crest line of the Himalayas. And the External Affairs Ministry-under the able guidance of its first Foreign Secretary K.P.S. Menon-made vigorous efforts to push the Indian administration into the NEFA area. Though the Chinese maps showed the boundary in this region along the foothills of Assam, the Chinese Government had no direct claim to any part of the NEFA area. Also by virtue of their suzerainty over Tibet, they could advance their claim only to Walong and Tawang in this region. According to Dr Alastair Lamb, "Apart from its inclusion within India of Tawang and Walong, the McMahon Line conflicted surprisingly little with Tibetan concepts as to their sphere of influence" (*The China-India Border*, p. 151). Tawang was a part of the Tsona district in Tibet and hundreds of monks in its great monastery were closely connected to Drepung Monastery in Lhasa, which was a major force in Tibetan politics. On the other hand the Tawang region was of special strategic importance to India, lying along the eastern boundary of Bhutan. Also through the Tawang Tract, which extended from the Tibetan plateau right down to Assam plains just north of Udalgiri, ran an important trade route between India and Tibet. The Government of India under the British Raj had taken Walong in 1943 and were trying to push administration into the tribal territories north of the foothills, gradually. But they more or less gave up the project of pushing administration upto the McMahon Line in the Tawang Tract, because of its incompatibility with their overall objective of drawing Tibet into the British sphere of influence and bolstering up Tibet as a friendly 'buffer state' against China. But Nehru and his intimate advisers on foreign policy—such as Sardar K. M. Panikkar, the first Indian Ambassador to the People's Republic of China—came to the conclusion that "the British policy (which we were supposed to have inherited) of looking upon Tibet as an area in which we had special political interests *could not be maintained*" (K. M. Panikkar : *In Two Chinas*, page 102). So unlike the British, free India was in a better position to take over the Tawang Tract by force from the Tibetan Government, provided such action did not lead to the Chinese intervention in the matter. It is to the credit of the External Affairs Ministry under the Secretaryship of K. P. S. Menon that the taking over of Tawang was planned during January-February 1951, when China was locked in grim battle in Korea with the American forces under the U.N. flag, and also there was a complete deadlock in Sino-Tibetan relations. The friendly attitude taken by India in regard to Communist China's claim to occupy the seat of China as a permanent member of the Security Council in preference to the Taiwan Government, as also India's recognition of the vital interest of China in the security of North Korea, together with India's disavowal of political interests in Tibet created an atmosphere of close understanding between India and China at that period. And so free India was able to accomplish the incorporation of the Tawang Tract, which was of vital strategic importance to her without a murmur from the Government of China. Of course, many areas of the North-east Frontier Agency remained unoccupied and unadministered till 1959, and even later, because of inaccessibility of the terrain and the difficulty of dealing with some of the wild tribes—living in the Hobbesian state of nature, owing no allegiance to any political authority. This was specially true of the Subansiri region, where members of the Thagin tribe murdered 73 Assam Rifles personnel in October 1953. Anyway, there was no protest from the Chinese side since 1950 upto the Tibetan uprising in March 1959 about the extension of the Indian Administration above the foothills of Assam by the People's Republic of China—which was in contrast with the attitude of the Nationalist Government of China during 1946-1949.

Conflict between India and China over the control of certain peripheral areas along the McMahon Line arose, only in the wake of the Tibetan revolt. On 15 December 1959, Nehru in a television interview with the veteran American journalist A. T. Steele gave a frank explanation of the cause of the sudden crisis, which had cropped up along the northern frontier in recent months. He said, "... the revolt in Tibet. That rather brought a certain speed in the events on our borders because the revolt in Tibet was being crushed by the Chinese forces and they naturally came to our borders where the fighting was on the other side. Tibetan refugees were coming in. They wanted to stop them, so they came to our border and a somewhat new situation arose for us in the last few months . . . *It was rather a succession of events which brought this conflict about.*" Dr A. S. Whiting wrote in 1963, "Had Tibet not erupted in revolt, no shooting might have occurred between the Indians and the Chinese. Instead, Peking probably would have continued to press quietly for its interpretation of the frontier." (A. S. Whiting : *Communist China* in *The Liberal Papers* Edited by James Roosevelt; page 298). Dr Alastair Lamb also finds the clue to the Sino-Indian border dispute in the eruption of the Tibetan revolt in March 1959, "Had it not been for the dramatic circumstances of the Tibetan revolt, this conflict of opinion (between India and China) would probably have given rise to little more than a continued exchange of notes". (*Indo-Tibetan Border, Australian Journal of Politics and History,* May 1960).

Anyway, if the Indian border-claims were limited to the Chinese recognition of the McMahon Line, it would not have resulted in an imbroglio, causing a costly confrontation along the extensive border stretching from Ladakh to NEFA for the last fourteen years. It is now definitely known from the testimony of K. P. S. Menon that when Chou En-lai visited India in April 1960, he offered a formula for the settlement of the Sino-Indian frontier dispute, "under which the Chinese Government would recognise the McMahon Line once and for all in return for some recognition on our part of Chinese claims in the disputed Aksai Chin Area." (*Twilight in China* : page 260). Chou En-lai's statement in the press conference in New Delhi on 25 April 1960, made it clear that the border dispute in the Central sector was of no significance to him, implying his readiness to accept Indian claims in this sector also, as a part of the overall settlement of the boundary problem which would involve Indian recognition of the Chinese claims in the Aksai Chin area ensuring the security of the Sinkiang-Tibet highway.

K. P. S. Menon has been the most knowledgeable person among the Indian diplomats since the days of the British Raj, and he was speaking with unchallengeable authority when he made the following remarks in his address at the Convocation of the Indian School of International Studies, New Delhi, on 13 December 1969 referring to Chou En-lai's offer to recognise the McMahon Line in lieu of Indian recognition of Chinese claims in the 'disputed' Aksai Chin area. "I deliberately say 'disputed', because maps, treaties, agreements, and other documents on which both sides rely cannot be said to place the boundary, as conceived by either party, beyond the region of doubt or the need for negotiation. The watershed principle, on which we have heavily relied in other sectors of the frontier, is in the Aksai Chin area, not in our favour. Moreover, it cannot be forgotten that Aksai Chin is of no importance to India, whereas, to China, it is of the utmost importance because it is the link between two historically troublesome regions, Tibet and Sinkiang." (*The Sixties in Retrospect,* page 12). The disputed nature of the Aksai region, as we know, was admitted by Nehru himself in several speeches in Parliament in August, September 1959. The official Note, submitted by the Indian Ambassador G. Parthasarathi to the Chinese Vice-Minister for Foreign Affairs in Peking, includes the following reference to the Aksai Chin area : "It is now clear that the Chinese Government also claim this area as their territory. The question whether a particular area is Indian or Chinese territory is *a matter in dispute."* (*White Paper 1954-1959,* page 29). This was also a recognition of the disputed nature of the Aksai Chin area.

But, as we have seen, the Historical Division of the Indian External Affairs Ministry, misinformed our Government about the true legacy of the British Raj in regard to our border claims in the Western sector. In the case of the Eastern sector also, they failed to do home work and find out the spurious nature of the *Aitchison's Treaties* (Volume XIV), 1929 relating to Tibet, which (Sir) Olaf Caroe fabricated in 1938 in order to falsely assert that the Simla Convention covered both the Sino-Tibetan and Sino-Indian boundaries and to confirm that McMahon Line was a legal boundary. [If they had simply cared to look into the *Aitchison's Treaties* (Volume XII) relating to Assam, (page 100), 1931, they would have seen that the Tawang tract in at least its northern reaches was under the Tibetan administration during the days of the British Raj]. In the case of the Western sector, they completely ignored the *Aitchison's Treaties* relating to Kashmir (Volume XII, Part I, page 5, 1931) which says, "The northern as well as the eastern boundary of the Kashmir State is still undefined." The way in which the Historical Division of the External Affairs Ministry twisted the content of the letter of March 14, 1899, written by the British Minister in Peking Sir C. M. Macdonald to the Ministers of the Tsungli Yamen (Chinese Foreign Office), giving the boundary proposal for Kashmir, later known as the Macartney-Macdonald line, was disingenuous. (This important document relating to the Indian border claims in the Kashmir sector was misquoted in the following important official communications made by the Government of India during 1959-1961: (1) Nehru's letter to Chou En-Lai dated 26th September 1959; (2) Letter to the Editor, The Times (London) entitled *China-India Border Dispute* written by M. A. Husain, Acting High Commissioner for India, published on 27th November 1959 : (3) *Report of the Officials of the Government of India and the People's Republic of China on the Boundary Question* (Ministry of External Affairs, Government of India : February 1961), page 55 of the Report of the Indian Officials.

The Historical Division of the External Affairs Ministry also appears to be responsible for the misrepresentation that the adaptation of the John Ardagh Line east of the Karakoram Pass —as shown in the Survey of India maps since July 1954—represents the watershed between the Indus system in India and the Khotan system in China. If the officials concerned had done their homework, they would have noticed that in *The Imperial Gazetteer of India (1908)*, Volume XV, page 84, there is the following quotation about the watershed in that region : *"The Karakoram range* is of a far more complicated character. Broadly speaking, it is a continuation of the Hindukush, and *forms the watershed between the Central Asian drainage and the streams flowing into the Indian Ocean."*

The negative role of the Historical Division of the External Affairs Ministry in keeping the Government of India and the public completely misinformed as to the true border legacy has been a major cause of the continued stalemate over the issue of the Sino-Indian frontier. Professor Ramsay Muir's dictum "Bureaucracy is like fire—invaluable as a servant, ruinous when it becomes a master," is applicable to the Historical Division of our External Affairs Ministry, as they were able to hamstring Nehru's original diplomacy—working for a *modus vivendi* with China, solving the boundary problem on a compromise basis. An official decision to keep the records of the External Affairs Ministry dealing with the Sino-Indian frontier since 1914 out of bounds for independent scholars has helped them to maintain till to-day a curtain of ignorance on the true border legacy of the British Raj and the history of Sino-Indian frontier still remains hidden to most of us.

SINO-INDIAN RELATIONS (1947-59)
—A RETROSPECT

Since the Tibetan revolt in March 1959, leading to the flight of the Dalai Lama to India and the border incidents that same year at Longju in the N.E.F.A. area in August and at the Kongka Pass in Ladakh in October, Sino-Indian relations—which had been so long played up by both sides as being based on Panch Sheel—steadily deteriorated into a phase of bitter Cold War. Then an actual military invasion of the Indian border by China took place in October 1962. As a sequel to the those events, there was almost universal condemnation of the Government of India's policy of befriending China and recognising her sovereignty over Tibet. There was also public disapproval and anger about the policy of keeping the fact of Chinese penetrations into border areas secret from Parliament and the people till August 1959. We shall make an attempt here to set forth the background of our policy towards China from 1947 to 1959.

It seems that India's policy towards China was based on the following considerations : Both China and India as underdeveloped countries with huge man-power, large territories and natural resources would require a long period of peace for unhampered economic growth at a rapid rate to attain their full status as World Powers. Military adventurism on the part of either India or China would be extreme folly, vitally affecting their national interests. So friendship between India and China, who have about two thousand miles long border between them, is a *sine quo non* of Indian as well as Chinese foreign policy, specially in the formative period of the life of these great Asian republics.

Warnings

On the other hand, Kautilya—the ancient master of Statecraft in India—taught us about the potential enmity of a powerful neighbour. Sardar K. M. Panikkar pointed out in his book *The Future of South-East Asia* in 1943 that India had no future as a Continental Power, since the Heartland would be controlled by the U.S.S.R. and a regenerated China. Panikkar warned us, "The growth of China as a military power and the recent shifting of the bases of its economic and military organisation to the South-east create equally difficult problems for India". To compensate for the loss of the continental defence system set up by the British, he called for a common defence area among India, Pakistan and Burma, strengthened by co-operation with Britain. Unfortunately, due to the innate hostility of Pakistan towards India, such a common defence area could not be built up after independence. Panikkar also warned his countrymen that with the growth of air-power, the Himalayas could not be an effective barrier against a potential enemy from the north, unless it was possible to include the Tibetan plateau within them. ("The Himalayas and Indian Defence", *India Quarterly*, No. 2 & 3, 1947).

Chiang-Kai-Shek's China was a 'ramshackle power', and so it did not pose a great problem for Indian security. We find, however, during the short duration between the establishment of the Interim Government in India in September 1946 and December 1949, several points of friction arose between India and Nationalist (K.M.T.) China. In the Asian Relations Conference held in New Delhi in March-April 1947, the Chinese (K.M.T.) delegates strongly objected to the display of a map of Asia in which Tibet was shown to be a distinct territory outside China, and got the map removed. The Chinese Ambassador in India made representation to the Indian Government against the continuation of the services of Hugh Richardson in Tibet, who was formerly the British Indian Political Agent (an office of dubious legality) in Lhasa, whom he regarded as *persona non grata*. The Government of India, however, continued the services of this controversial British citizen in the Indian Foreign service till August 1949. Richardson was a champion of Tibetan independence, and the retention of his services in Lhasa till the eve of the Communist revolution in China, might be regarded as significant. The Chinese Ambassador (K.M.T.) objected to a map of Kashmir with its neighbour Tibet shown outside the Chinese boundary line, in a documentary film on Kashmir. On 18 November 1949, the Chinese Ambassador (K.M.T.) sent a Note saying that the Government of China did not recognise the McMahon Line. The delegate of China (K.M.T.) took a lukewarm attitude towards

Indian complaint in the Security Council about the tribal invasion of Kashmir and Pakistan's complicity in it. On the issue of the Dutch aggression on Indonesia—against which India tried to mobilise Asian opinion as also to move the Security Council—Nationalist China failed to respond favourably, presumably looking to the narrow self-interest of the overseas 'Chinese traders in Indonesia. The rampant corruption in Nationalist China, combined with authoritarianism and misrule was too well-known. The big-brotherly attitude shown by some Nationalist Chinese diplomats towards the Indian delegates in the U.N. and elsewhere was irritating.

Early Fears

On 23 April 1949, when the Chinese Communist forces crossed the river Yangshi and captured Nanking, the gateway to South China was opened to the Red Army and the fate of the Nationalist Government could be taken as sealed. In the Commonwealth Prime Ministers' conference held in London on 27th April, 1949, Nehru made known his decision to remain within the Commonwealth on the basis of a compromise formula. Considering the strength of the anti-Commonwealth sentiment prevalent in India, forcefully subscribed to by Nehru himself in the recent past (Cf. *Discovery of India* : 1945), the Government of India's decision to maintain close ties with Britain through the Commonwealth was influenced at least partially by the vision of the rise of the Red Star over China.

The Government of India initiated some diplomatic measures in the peripheral areas of China in the interest of Indian security at about this time. On 6 June 1949, following a period of tension between the Maharajah of Sikkim and the interim Government led by the Sikkim Congress, H. Dayal, the Indian Political Officer, took over the administration of Sikkim at the request of the Maharajah. Later on, an Indian Administrator assumed the charge of administration. (A new treaty confirming the protectorate status of Sikkim was signed on 5 December, 1950). On 8 August 1949, India signed a new treaty with Bhutan under which Bhutan undertook to be guided by India in foreign affairs. In July 1949, the Chinese (K.M.T.) Mission in Lhasa was made to leave via India by the Tibetan Government on a specious plea. Complicity of Hugh Richardson, the Head of the Indian Mission in Lhasa, was suspected in this matter by the Nationalist Government of China. (T. T. Li, *Tibet-To-day and Yesterday*, p. 199). H. Dayal visited Lhasa sometime later. India agreed to supply arms and ammunition to the Tibetan Government. The Tibetan Government, however, did not commit themselves to a thoroughgoing training programme by Indian military officers. (H. Richardson, *Tibet And Its History*, p. 178). The British Government of India had started developing administrative centres in NEFA since 1943, and this policy was seriously pursued by the Nehru Government. The Government of India also supplied small arms to the Government of Burma in 1949, when it was facing a Communist rebellion. India also arranged for a Commonwealth loan to be paid to Burma at this time. Nehru, while championing colonial liberation movement in Asia, condemned the Chinese-led movement against the British in Malaya in June 1950 as sheer terrorism and allowed the transit of Gurkha troops from Nepal to Malaya through India. It appears that Nehru was quite conscious of the danger arising out of the existence of a Communist Chinese base at the gateway of the Indian Ocean.

On the other hand, the Government of India gave recognition to the Chinese People's Republic on 30th December, 1949, within three months of its establishment, Nehru, during his visit to Britain and America in October 1949, pleaded with both the Governments for an early recognition of the Communist regime in China, as he considered it to be a stable regime enjoying the allegiance of a vast body of population in China. Since January 1950, the Government of India consistently pleaded in the U.N. for a delegate of the People's Republic of China being seated in the position due to China as a permanent member of the Security Council, in place of the Nationalist delegate.

THE KOREAN EPISODE

On 25 June 1950, when the war started in Korea, India was alone among the uncommitted Powers in the Security Council to join the Western Powers to condemn this as a case of aggression from Communist North Korea (Yugoslavia and Egypt abstained). India also supported the military action initiated by President Truman against North Korea in the name of the U.N. On the other hand, India expressed inability to provide any military contingent to the U.N. army in Korea. More than that, on 13th July, 1950, Nehru sent personal messages to Stalin and Acheson (U.S. Secretary of State) pleading for an early mediation to stop the bloodshed in Korea, and he stressed therein the necessity of the presence of the Soviet Union and the People's Republic of China in the Security Council, the two Great Powers bordering on Korea. (The Soviet Union had been boycotting the Security Council meetings on the issue of Chinese representation since 13th January, 1950, and this had helped the Western Powers in bypassing the Veto and launching a military action against North Korea under the banner of the U.N.). Nehru had, earlier, dissociated himself from President Truman's declaration about the so-called 'neutralisation' of Formosa and arms-aid to the French in fighting the Communist-led Vietminh forces in Indo-China. This declaration had been made along with Truman's order to deploy the American army in support of the Republic of Korea on 27 June 1950.

In October 1950, when the U.N. army under American leadership decided to cross the 38th parallel and invade North Korea, Nehru strongly opposed the action. Apart from the moral ground, Nehru was convinced that the invasion of North Korea was bound to result in the Chinese intervention and this might lead to an extension of the conflict in the Far East. It was at this time, that the Government of Communist China ordered the Army to move into Tibet when they found that the Tibetan delegates were procrastinating for more than six months, staying within India on their journey to Peking for a political settlement. India made strong protests to China on the issue of sending an army into Tibet and made it an occasion to remind China about certain privileges in Tibet which the Government of India had inherited from the British days. Though Communist China resented this diplomatic interference by India in the matter of Tibet, the Chinese Army halted after the fall of Chamdo on the Eastern border of Tibet. The Government of India also did not try to dissuade the Tibetans from going to Peking as they (G.O.I.) had implicitly warned in their letter to China on 31 October 1950. Apart from this episode about Tibet, there was practically no point of serious dispute between India and China till the end of the Korean war in July 1953.

New Power Balance

On the other hand, the collapse of General MacArthur's offensive in November 1950 in face of the massive attack by the ill-equipped Chinese infantry, and President Truman's talk about the possibility of dropping the Atom bomb in Korea, stimulated anti-Western feelings throughout Asia. Speaking in Parliament on 6 and 7 December, 1950, Nehru condemned both sides in the Korean War for being responsible for the genocide of a small Asian nation in the name of freedom and unity of Korea. Nehru was by then conscious of the shift in the world balance of power caused by the emergence of China as a formidable Power able to face the American challenge in Asia, as also of the advantageous position gained by India in holding a middle-ground in the new power balance.

Definitive Frontier

At the same time, Nehru thought that the time was ripe to let China know definitely what India considered to be her legitimate border and sphere of influence, and which she was ready to defend by all means. Already on 20 November 1950, Nehru chose to reiterate the statement that "Map or no map, the McMahon Line is our definitive frontier". On December 6, Nehru repeated an earlier statement that the Himalayas formed India's traditional northern frontier and that since Nepal was on this side of the Himalayas, any threat to the security of Nepal would be considered a threat to India's security. (Already on 3 July 1950, a Treaty of Friendship between India and Nepal had been signed). In December 1950, the Government of India took concrete steps to get democratic reforms introduced in Nepal, as the continuation of a corrupt and inefficient Rana oligarchy was a threat to Nepal's stability as well as India's security. On the Tibetan appeal to the U.N. for aid against Chinese 'aggression' made on 13 November 1950, the Government of India have no support, as they had been assured by Communist China of a peaceful settlement on the question of Tibetan autonomy.* The

---

* The Government of India's view on the Tibetan complaint about aggression against China was undoubtedly influenced by her own attitude towards the complaint about aggression against herself by Hyderabad, submitted to the Security Council in July 1948.

North and North-eastern Border Committee was established in February 1951 under the Chairmanship of General Himmat Singhji to consider the question of security of our border areas.

On 1 February 1951, India firmly opposed the U.S. sponsored resolution in the U.N. General Assembly calling China an aggressor. The Sino-Tibetan agreement was signed in Peking on 23 May 1951. Since 1951, there started an exchange of visits between India and China by goodwill and cultural missions, and this fostered mutual understanding. China apparently appreciated India's role as a mediator in the Korean war which had turned into a bloody stalemate by this time. Nehru's criticism of the American-sponsored Japanese Treaty signed in September 1951, on the ground that the treaty failed to restore Formosa to China, as well as on other grounds such as the continuance of American bases in Japan, was agreeable to China. The Indian formula for solving the suestion of repatriation of prisoners of war had originally received tacit consent from the Chinese, and it provoked sharp criticism from the U. S. A. when circulated in the U. N. Assembly in October 1952. Krishna Menon was induced by Anthony Eden (British Foreign Minisster) to accept certain amendments to meet the American point of view. This, in its turn, made the Indian formula suspect in the Soviet and Chinese eyes, and they vehemently opposed the Indian resolution on P.O.W's in the U.N. This misunderstanding was, however, short-lived. The acceptance of the original Indian plan by Red China as the basis of a Korean armistice in July 1953, coupled with American insistence on the exclusion of India from the proposed Political Conference on the Far Eastern settlement, on the specious ground of her being a non-belligerent, brought India and China nearer to each other.

Tibet

The next phase in Sino-Indian relations was the initiative taken by India to regularise her position in Tibet, by giving up the few extra-territorial rights she had inherited from the British regime, which were in themselves of little value to India, (H. Richardson : *A Short History of Tibet*, p. 198) and which also could not be maintained in the changed context of power relationship. On 29 April 1954, the Sino-Indian Agreement was signed. The central provisions of the Agreement dealt with the number, location and regulation of trade markets, routes and procedure for trade and pilgrimage. The treaty provisions were supplemented by a Note dealing with the withdrawal of Indian military escorts and the handing over of Indian post and telegraph facilities and of the Indian rest-houses in Tibet to the Chinese. The most important element in the Treaty was, however, contained within the preamble in which Tibet was referred as "The Tibet Region of China". This was a definite assurance to China, that India—once for all—had declared the old British policy over Tibet. On the other hand, the Five Principles of Coexistence contained in the preamble of the 1954 Agreement provided a sort of reassurance of Communist China's peaceful intent toward India. Critics in India, such as Dr H. Kunzru M.P. (Rajya Sabha), raised the question after the border clashes had occurred in August and October 1959 : "When the Panch Sheel agreement was made between India and China under this agreement, we recognised Tibet as a region of China. Could we not on this occasion at least have said to the Chinese Government, "If you want us to agree to these words, you should at least recognise the McMahon Line ?" It transpires from Nehru's speech in the Rajya Sabha on 9 December 1959, that while India was merely accepting the reality of the Chinese occupation of Tibet —which she was not in a position to alter—the raising of the claim for the McMahon Line border across the table would have led to a demand for a *quid pro quo* by Communist China (on the basis of the Chinese (K.M.T.) Note rejecting the McMahon Line as late as 18 November 1949).

India's Predicament

The Government of India felt that it would be better to make our position about the McMahon Line clear in our maps and declarations in Parliament, and hold by our position firmly, and allow *"the lapse of time and events",* (Nehru's speech in the Rajya Sabha on 9 December 1959, Prime Minister on *Sino-Indian Relations,* Vol. 1. p. 250), to vindicate our claim in this sector of the boundary along the high crest of the Himalayas—the natural geographic frontier of India. Anyway, it would be clear to anybody who cared to study the Indian official maps current in December 1953—when the negotiations started—that it might have resulted in opening up a hornet's nest at a time, when India was eager to build friendly relations with Red China in the context of the Pak-American Arms Aid Pact negotiations started in November 1953. In fact, the coming to power of the Republican party in the U.S.A. in 1953, meant that the influence of the China Lobby, who were pledged to roll back 'the mud-tide of Communism' in Asia through armed intervention, was ascendent in American politics.

Asian Peace

In January 1954, Robertson, the U.S. Assistant Secretary of State, was reported as making a statement about the American desire to dominate the Far East, which no Indian could relish. On 24 February 1954, the Pak-American Military Pact was signed. Then came in quick succession the Dulles doctrine of 'massive atomic retaliation' in any place of America's own choosing in case of any nibbling attack by Communists anywhere, and the precipitous American attempt to press for a massive Western intervention in Indo-China in April 1954 on the eve of the Geneva Conference, (which might have started a fresh trail of turmoil in the Far East). For obvious reasons, the Government of India tried to build the ramparts of the Asian peace on the basis of Sino-Indian understanding.

It is only in this context that we can understand Nehru's eagerness to invite Chou En-lai in June 1954 and to sign a joint statement eulogising the principles of peaceful co-existence between two states following divergent ideologies. By such a joint statement, Nehru was insisting upon a policy of extension of the 'peace area', devoid of cold war, as opposed to the pactomania of the U.S.A. which led to continuous accretion of military power to Pakistan.

China's attitude in the Geneva Conference 1954 as well as in the Afro-Asian Conference at Bandung in 1955 was quite conciliatory, and impressed the Governments of Afro-Asian countries. As a result the SEATO (1954) and the Baghdad Pact (1955) had no real basis in Asian support. India's genuine efforts to narrow down the points of conflict between Communist China and the U.S.A. during the period from 1955 to 1958 (e.g. the release of Chinese citizens in the U.S.A., the release of American flyers arrested for espionage in China, the crises about off-shore islands in 1955 and August 1958) as also her constant pleading for the entry of Red China in the U.N. were appreciated by the Chinese leaders. During his visit to India in the winter of 1956-57, Chou En-lai paid high tributes to the Indian leaders for the diplomatic support given on various issues and openly confessed that China had much to learn from India in the organisation of Science and Industry.

The question of Chinese maps, which showed some parts of our extensive border region within the Chinese territory from the time of Chiang-Kai-shek, should have been a cause of headache to the Indian Government right from the date of transfer of power in 1947. But as China remained a weak power till the end of 1949, the Government of India, like its predecessor the British Government, bothered little about the tall claims made in Chinese maps. It was on 8 February 1950, that for the first time Nehru spoke in Parliament about the McMahon Line being India's northern frontier. He also repeated several times in the same year, that the Himalayas were the natural frontier of India and, as such, Nepal was included in the defence perimeter of India.

The Map Controversy

Nehru first raised the question of Chinese maps with Chou En-lai in October, 1954. He received the reply that the new Red China maps were copied from the old K.M.T. maps and did not signify a definitive border alignment. During Chou En-lai's visit to India in the winter of 1956-57, Nehru and Chou discussed the question of McMahon Line again, in connection with the settlement of the Burma border. Nehru had discussed the Burma border in a letter to Chou En-lai in 1956, presumably because he thought that a satisfactory solution of the Burma border on the basis of the McMahon Line would strengthen India's position about the remaining section of that Line. Anyway, according to Nehru's testimony, Chou En-lai's talks with him contained a tacit acceptance of the McMahon Line "in consideration of the friendly relations between India and China." Nehru was satisfied, and did not raise the other territorial disputes along the Central and Western sections of the Northern border. Perhaps due to lack of proper definitions of the border in those sectors in the Survey of India maps issued before July 1954, Nehru did not think it politic to raise the question. (Also the Government of India had, by its own commitment in the U.N., left the future of the Kashmir State somewhat open, and hence weakened its case about the Kashmir boundary).

THE KHAMPA EPISODE

Since the end of 1955, the Khampas, a warlike Tibetan-speaking tribe who were residents of the Szechuan province outside the Tibetan boundary, rose in revolt against the Communist rule. As the Khampas owed spiritual allegiance to the Dalai Lama, he was put under pressure by the Chinese to control the revolt. Caught between two fires, the Dalai Lama, who was on a visit to India in the winter of 1956-57, decided to stay back till he could regain the autonomy enjoyed by his predecessor, the 13th Dalai Lama. Nehru tried hard to bring a reconciliation between Chou En-lai and the Dalai Lama, as he knew all along that it was the only guarantee for security and tranquillity to India's sprawling northern border. As the neutralisation of the south and south-west border of China was of vital interest to Red China—which was faced in the East and South-East by powerful American bases—Chou En-lai showed a conciliatory attitude and arranged for the withdrawal of Communist reforms from Tibet proper, withdrew a large body of political cadres and closed down the Chinese language schools set up in Tibet. There were practically no border probings by the Chinese along the Himalayan frontier in 1957. In September 1957, however, the Government of India learnt from an announcement by the Chinese Government that a motor road had been constructed from Yehcheng to Gartok through the Aksai Chin area. But the Government of India waited till 18 October 1958 to submit an informal note of protest on that issue. This note was written with a view to seeking the release of one of the Army patrols (sent in the summer of 1958 for verifying the alignment of the Sinkiang-Tibet road), who were presumably in the Chinese custody. This

Note also stated *inter alia* : "The Government of India are anxious to settle these *petty frontier disputes* so that friendly relations between the countries may not suffer." The Chinese Government released and deported the Indian patrol through the Karakoram pass on October 22, but they protested against Indian personnel conducting unlawful surveys within Chinese territory. A note submitted by the Indian Ambassador on 8 November 1958, tacitly accepted the existence of a territorial dispute in this region. Already on 21 August 1958, the Government of India had written a Note objecting to the boundary of China with India as shown in a map published in *The China Pictorial,* July 1958. In this Note, for the first time objection was taken about large areas of eastern Ladakh being shown as Chinese territory*. (Before this, the Government of India showed concern about only the McMahon Line border). The Chinese Note of 3 November 1958 referred to *The China Pictorial* map as a 'rough sketch map' drawn on the basis of pre-Liberation period maps, but said that changes in the boundary would be made only after consultations with neighbouring countries and a survey of the border regions.

Growing Concern

On 14 December 1958, Nehru (on his return from a visit to Bhutan) personally wrote to Chou En-lai a long letter on the issue of 'incorrect Chinese maps', specially objecting to a large part of the NEFA (McMahon Line sector) being shown as part of China. He referred to the possibility of grave misunderstanding which might arise between the two countries out of this. He also expressed inability to understand "what kind of surveys can affect these well-known and fixed boundaries," On January 23, 1959, Chou En-Lai in his reply to Nehru stressed the point that "the Sino-Indian boundary has never been formally delimited". He specially objected to the way the Sino-Indian boundary was shown in the western section in Indian maps. On the McMahon Line, however, he thought it necessary to "take a more or less realistic attitude." But he reiterated the need for proper consultation and surveys, and pointed out that an immediate change

---

* A protest had been made on July 2 about the visit of the Chinese troops to Khurnak post in eastern Ladakh.

might create political difficulties for the Chinese Government and proposed as a provisional measure, the maintenance of the *status quo*.

Worsening Relations

This embryonic border dispute between India and China had been there for a long time, and negotiations were being carried through privately by the Foreign Ministry officials and the Prime Ministers of India and China. But on no side there was any feeling of basic hostility towards the other. Unlike the Indo-Pakistan boundaries where the bulk of the Indo-Pakistan armies stood face to face, and firings along the frontiers were a frequent phenomenon, the Sino-Indian border along the length of more than 1500 miles (leaving the Nepal border) was not manned by armed forces on either side—except at a few strategic points. There was almost absolute tranquility along the border though very minor disputes, some left over by history (e.g. Barahoti) or others arising out of the survey operations in hitherto unexplored regions, became subjects of official Notes since July 1954. But the political developments in Tibet since the summer of 1958, contributed to a rapid worsening in Sino-Indian relations and made the solution of the border dispute politically difficult for both the Governments, more so for the Government of India, as the expression of public opinion was much more free in India than in China. As late as 21 October 1959, at a press conference at Calcutta, Nehru said that he did not think that there was any "major idea" behind the recent Chinese incursions into Indian territory. He added, "I am inclined to think that all these were tagged to Tibet. There were no Chinese forces on the other side of the border before the Tibetan rebellion. But after the rebellion, Chinese forces came partly to crush the rebellion and partly to stop the Tibetan people from coming over to India, or contact the people whom the Chinese imagined to be connected with the Tibetan rebellion". Again in December 1959, in an exclusive interview with the veteran American journalist, A. T. Steele, Nehru said, ". . . . that (the Tibetan revolt) rather brought about a certain speed in the events in our borders, because the revolt in Tibet was being crushed by the Chinese forces and they naturally came to our border where the fighting was on the other side".

In answer to the question, "What is the basic reason that impels China to put pressure on India?", Nehru said, "I am not myself sure that this was very deliberate on their part. It was rather a succession of events which brought the conflict about."*

Nehru's efforts to bring about a conciliation between the Dalai Lama and the Chinese Government was apparently successful in 1957, when the Dalai Lama went back to Lhasa in spite of persuasions by his elder brothers, and Mao Tse-tung declared in a speech in February 1957 that Tibet was not yet ready for reforms and that reforms should be postponed for six years. But as the reforms were being withdrawn from the region of Tibet, they were being forcibly introduced in the outlying areas where the bulk of the Khampa tribe lived as minorities in the Szechuan province. As a result the Khampas took the path of rebellion again in the spring of 1958.

Chinese Plans

The Chinese wanted that the Dalai Lama's Government should send its army to quell the rebellion, but the Dalai Lama did not co-operate. The Dalai Lama sent some emissaries to the Khampa areas in an attempt to bring about a peaceful settlement of the dispute. But somehow, his emissaries decided to make a common cause with the Khampas, and in July 1958 they made a call for the independence of Greater Tibet, including the areas in China inhabited by the Tibetan minorities. This joint manifesto of Tibetan independence was also signed by Lukhangwa the ex-Prime Minister of Tibet demoted by the Chinese authorities in 1953, as also by other Tibetan nobles living in exile in the Indian

---

* (1) The emerging Sino-Indian conflict arising out of a difficult border legacy left by the British was clearly foreseen by Guy Wint in the article "The Challenge of Tibet", *The Round Table*, June 1959. (2) "Had it not been for the dramatic circumstances of the *Tibetan revolt*, this conflict of opinion (between India and China) would probably have given rise to little more than a continued exchange of notes"—vide Alastair Lamb, "The Indo-Tibetan Border", *The Australian Journal of Politics*, May 1960. (3) "Had Tibet not erupted in revolt, no shooting might have occurred between Indians and Chinese. Instead, Peking probably would have continued to press quietly for its interpretation of the frontier"—A. S. Whiting, "Communist China", *The Liberal Papers* edited by James Roosevelt (1963).

border town Kalimpong, and through them it received wide publicity causing a loss of face to the Chinese Government. Since then, the Government of China harboured a lingering doubt as to how far the Government of India was earnest in checking the anti-Chinese activities of the Tibetan nobles, K.M.T. agents and other western people, resident in Kalimpong. (During his visit to India in November 1956, Chou En-Lai, apparently, made a request for the removal of Prince Peter of Greece from Kalimpong. Prince Peter had been given a notice to quit India in early 1957, but he managed to extend his stay in Kalimpong on the plea of his wife's illness till early 1959).

The principal strategy of the Tibetan rebels was to spirit away the Dalai Lama out of the reach of the Chinese and make him the symbol of national revolt and then seek for foreign intervention. Alternatively, the Chinese authorities had a plan to move away the Dalai Lama out of the reach of the Tibetan rebels. Ultimately the Tibetan rebels won the battle of wits, and managed to convince the Dalai Lama that it was time to part from the Chinese and escape to India. This dramatic flight of the Dalai Lama to India, and the subsequent moves taken by him and his supporters in India, and the simultaneous setting in of chain reactions in China, suddenly brought to light all the skeletons in the cupboard, which had been so long hidden from the public eye by the Indian as well as the Chinese Government with a view to stabilising their relations on a friendly basis amid their gigantic tasks of national reconstruction, and the looming danger of hostile operations from Pakistan (armed with U.S. weapons), and the U.S.A. respectively.

THE SINO-INDIAN DISPUTE

A meeting some time back was held in an Arab country between the official representatives of Peking and New Delhi for exploring the ways and means for normalisation of Sino-Indian relations. Points raised by China in this meeting as reported by one correspondent of a leading Indian Daily then staying at Beirut were as follows :

(1) One of the conditions is the Chinese insistence that India must recognise the Aksai Chin region as an integral part of China. (2) The second condition is that the two countries should reach an agreement on a new delineation of the frontiers replacing the McMahon Line. (3) Another Chinese demand is the withdrawal of Indian support for Tibetan emigrants, which would mean the expulsion of the Dalai Lama and other leaders of the Tibetan nationalist movement from the Indian territory. (4) Also China wants India to stop all military intervention in Bangladesh and to withdraw its troops from that country. (5) China's last condition is that India should officially and publicly declare that her treaty of friendship with the U.S.S.R. does not contain any secret clause. (*The Statesman,* 9 February 1973).

It would, therefore, be correct in asserting that there is not much that was new in the conditions reported to have been submitted by the Chinese for normalisation of relations. The new conditions were (4) and (5), which arose out of the events such as the signing of the Indo-Soviet Treaty on 9th August, 1971, and the Indo-Pakistan War in December, 1971, leading to the dismemberment of Pakistan and the emergence of the Bangladesh as a sovereign state. I would like to limit my comments to the older issues in the Sino-Indian dispute.

Thanks to Kuldip Nayar, we have an eye-witness account of the conversations that took place between Chou En-lai and the late G. B. Pant in April, 1960, during the Chinese Prime Minister's visit to New Delhi to resolve the Sino-Indian dispute. Nayar wrote, "Until then my impression had been that the dispute was only about the Ladakh side, but Chou En-lai twice or thrice questioned the validity of the McMahon Line. Pant began with the presumption that the McMahon Line was a settled fact, but Chou En-lai did not accept this. He made it quite clear that McMahon Line was open to interpretation.

"Chou En-lai explained how important for China was the road it had built to join Sinkiang with Tibet. Without that road China had no way of reaching Sinkiang, he argued. Pant's reply was that India was ready to guarantee safe and free traffic between Tibet and Sinkiang, but would not part with its territory. Chou En-lai kept quiet, but he did hint at consequences fraught with danger." (*Between the Lines*, p. 137).

Nayar also refers to the negotiations to settle the Sino-Indian dispute that took place in Geneva between Krishna Menon, India's Defence Minister, and Chen Yi, China's Foreign Minister, in Geneva in July, 1962, and says, "Menon had told Chen Yi... that India might accept China's suzerainty over the area in Aksai Chin where it had built the road to link Sinkiang and Tibet as well as over a ten-mile strip to serve as 'buffer' to the road. In exchange, China must officially accept the McMahon Line and India's right to the rest of Ladakh. China had reportedly accepted this and so had Menon who apparently had talked to Nehru before going to Geneva. But Pant reportedly stood in the way and had the Government withdraw its offer through an informal resolution in the Cabinet." (*Ibid*, p. 136).

I would say that it is time now that the Government of India under Nehru's daughter, who is more a realist than starry-eyed in external affairs, should take up the threads of the last bilateral discussions between India and China held in Geneva in July, 1962. Recent researches by scholars such as Alastair Lamb, Dorothy Woodman, Neville Maxwell as well as myself on the sources of Sino-Indian dispute show that the late Prime Minister Nehru, who had originally put great stress on a policy of Sino-Indian amity on the basis of realism, was forced to take a rigid posture about the Northern border since November, 1959, which was not warranted by facts of history. It was a pity that Nehru —then an old man of 70—was surrounded by some diplomats whose professional acumen and integrity were not what should have been, and a little later he was under the spell of the same type of military officials who encouraged him to the path of military confrontation with China in utter disregard to the strategic realities. It should be clear by now to the Government of India that the Indian claim to Aksai Chin had no basis in treaty, usage or in geography—such as the water-shed principle. While India's claim to the McMahon Line has a firm basis in geography as well as usage, it has no basis in a valid international treaty.

On scrutiny of the wide variety of maps published by the Governments of India and China, Miss Dorothy Woodman, who was a geographer by training, concluded "...any settlement of the Sino-Indian Border involves compromise." Miss Woodman found fault with both sides in this respect. She said, "... the innumerable discrepancies in maps might lead the most naive student of cartography to the view that the devil can quote the maps to serve his own purpose." (*Himalayan Frontier,* p. 320). She suggested a possible line of settlement of the dispute based on compromise : "The fact that China accepted the Red Line of 1914 Simla Tripartite maps in her discussion with Burma, suggests that this might be a starting point in the case of India." (*Ibid,* p. 321). On the other hand, she thought that India should limit her claim in the Aksai Chin sector to the Macartney-Macdonald Line of 1899, then accepted by Sinkiang officials but not endorsed by Nanking. In fact, Miss Woodman came to the conclusion that the starting point of a Sino-Indian rapprochement would be the formula supposed to have been suggested by Chou En-lai to Nehru in April, 1960. K. P. S. Menon, the Indian diplomat now in retirement, also commended this formula in his book, *The Flying Troika.*

I would, however, suggest that the border question should be the last item in any meaningful Sino-Indian dialogue, as the problem has become most complicated being mixed up with the politics of prestige. Negotiations should better start aiming at such limited but essential objectives as the following :

(1) Agreement on complete stoppage of hostile propaganda by India and China through the Press and the Radio. This should include stoppage of publication of official notes—which have been a continuing source of friction between the two countries. This has been more or less implemented informally in recent months.

(2) Appointment of Ambassadors in Peking and New Delhi. On restoring ambassadorial relations China may want India to take the first step, contending that the Indian Ambassador was the first to be recalled. Any initiative in this respect from the

side of India, as it seems, will now be reciprocated from the Chinese side.

(3) There should be complete withdrawal of clandestine support from the dissident minority groups such as, Tibetans, Naga and Mizo rebels, 'Azad Kashmir' protagonists—who played no mean part in aggravating the dimensions of Sino-Indian conflict.

(4) Re-opening of mutually beneficial Trans-Himalayan trade on a new treaty basis and gradual softening of the disputed border with growth of confidence between the two countries.

SINO-INDIAN RELATIONS—THE PROSPECTS OF A DETENTE

The Indian Press in the recent past (1973, Summer) published several news items which would indicate that the Government of India has been particularly anxious to normalise relations with the People's Republic of China. We may for example refer to Mrs Indira Gandhi's interview in New Delhi with the Australian Broadcasting Commission on 26 May 1973, and her interviews to the Belgrade Television and the Canadian Television during her itineraries in June 1973. At the same time we find that there has been little progress during the last few years in the process of normalisation in India-China relations, in spite of the flickers of hope caused by statements of the Prime Minister and the Foreign Minister of India, which they have been repeating time and again since early 1969.

India and China did not break off diplomatic relations but have been maintaining barely a skeleton staff in their respective Embassies since 1962. The Trade and Pilgrimage Treaty of 1954 was allowed to lapse in June 1962, when India spurned the Chinese request for fresh negotiations for a new treaty. Thus the Indian and Chinese Consulates were closed down and the regular flow of Trans-Himalayan trade and pilgrimage which have been a source of income to the people in the Himalayan border region came to a sudden halt. The Indian Ambassador left Peking in the spring of 1961 and never returned to his post in Peking, while the Chinese Ambassador was withdrawn from India in the summer of 1962. Since then the respective Embassies remained under the respective *Charge dé Affaires*.

Even in the worst days of the Cold War, the U.S.A. and the Soviet Union maintained Ambassadors in Moscow and Washington. East and West Germany, the two bitter contestants in the Cold War—even when they did not accord official recognition to each other,—allowed a large volume of trade between themselves. On the other hand, India and China who in 1954 professed to be eternal friends turned within a short period of five years into 'eternal enemies', and relations remained thoroughly poisoned due to such happenings as the Tibetan revolt, the frontier dispute, the Chinese border invasion of 1962, alleged support to the dissident minorities such as the Tibetans, Nagas and the Mizos, Azad Kashmiris by India or China, and the psychological warfare carried through the press and the radio by either side. During 1967 there were raids in our Peking Embassy and manhandling of Indian diplomats by the Chinese youth, and retaliatory action in New Delhi. In 1967, there were also armed clashes in the Sikkim border in September/October.

After three years of the Cultural Revolution, China was gradually recovering her diplomatic sanity since 1969, and after the Sino-Soviet clash at Ussuri, China became conscious of the need for normalisation of her relations with outside world. At a May Day reception in Peking in 1970, Mao Tse-tung made a friendly gesture to the Indian Charge dé Affaires Brajesh Misra. Since then, the Chinese have been less cold and more correct in their attitude towards India, attending our National Day functions in New Delhi and other important capitals. But there were no definite gestures to show that China was too eager to mend her fences with India in the immediate future. China's main headache in the recent past has been the aggravation of the Sino-Soviet dispute. The Sino-American rapprochement, the signing of the Armistice to close the war in Vietnam, the renewal of Sino-Japanese ties burying the bitterness of a protracted Japanese invasion of the mainland China in the thirties and later, also her entry as a recognised Great Power into the United Nations in October 1971 after 22 years of isolation—these have been the major preoccupations as well as achievements of Chinese diplomacy since the fading out of the Cultural Revolution. China's interest in attaining a settlement in the Far East and South-East Asia would naturally be much greater than attaining a settlement in South Asia, which involves an improvement of relations with India. On the other hand, after the break-up of Pakistan and the emergence of Bangladesh in December 1971, a settlement with China on an equitable basis remains the first priority for Indian diplomacy so that we may stabilise our position as the dominant power in South Asia. Thus on the basis of logical thinking, we find that the initiative for a detenté in Sino-Indian relations should come from the Indian side.

There are, however, certain major obstacles in the way of opening a serious dialogue with China after a decade of cold war. The public opinion in India has for long been fed with official and unofficial propaganda about the Chinese betrayal of India's genuine friendship and her 'unprovoked aggression' against our country in 1962. The Indian public was also fed with propaganda about the sacrosant nature of our Northern boundary being in the Himalayas. As a result, it may still be allergic to any mutual adjustment of boundary claims between India and China on a give-and-take basis. The Sino-Indian impasse cannot be satisfactorily tackled before a serious effort is made by the Indian Government in re-educating the public opinion about the sources of the Sino-Indian dispute as it developed during 1958-1962, suddenly reversing the trend of co-operative and peaceful co-existence. Again, the Indo-Soviet Treaty of 9 August 1971 might be an inhibiting factor in the process of normalisation of relations with China. According to a recent study by an Indian publicist, the Sino-Indian dispute is but a function of the more complicated Sino-Soviet dispute, and it would be futile to expect a normalisation of our relations until there is a detenté in Sino-Soviet relations (Mohan Ram : *Sino-Indian Confrontation;* 1973). A school of thought still flourishes in India, which thinks that India should aim at the re-establishment of Tibet as a buffer state between India and China (B. M. Mullik : *My Years With Nehru,* p. 613). This would, however mean the maintenance of a permanent military confrontation along the 2000-mile northern border of India. There are others who still insist that India can have fresh dialogue with China only on the basis of her acceptance of the Colombo proposals of 1963, which envisaged setting up of civilian posts by both sides on mutual agreement in the area in the Western sector above the 1959, 7th November Line evacuated by the Chinese Army.

We have, however, several grounds for optimism about the prospects of a detenté. The psychosis of fear about China which persisted in early sixties has gradually evaporated by now. Our Army proved its mettle in the two wars, in 1965, and then in 1971, by which Pakistan has been cut to size. China provided merely verbal support to Pakistan in her hours of crisis. Thus there is no reason to think that China would remain our sworn enemy for ever, or that she has territorial designs south of the Himalayas. Also the process of Sino-American detenté, which started in July 1971 with the visit of President Nixon's special emissary Dr Kissinger to Peking, had a salutary effect on the powerful pro-American lobby operating in India. They had penetrated the Congress party hierarchy, the bureaucracy and the Press since the fifties, and persistently urged a militant no-compromise policy with Communist China till recently. Indira Gandhi may today even expect encouragement in her efforts for a Sino-Indian detenté from the same group of people, who hamstrung her father's original policy towards Communist China, which would have recognised Chinese claims over the Aksai Chin road on the far side of the Karakoram mountains in lieu of Chinese recognition of the McMahon Line in the eastern sector. The same, however, is not true of the Tibetan lobby which has also been quite active in India for many years trying to sow seeds of discord between India and China specially since 1959, when the Dalai Lama came to settle in India along with a large number of followers. There is indication that the Government of India are not going to give undue consideration to the claims of dissident minorities at the cost of a prospective detenté with China. The Taiwan lobby in India is dying a natural death. An improvement in Sino-Indian relations should be welcome to both the Super Powers to-day, if they are really earnest about burying the Cold War throughout the world and scaling down the crippling burden of the armaments race. The Indo-Soviet Treaty of 1971 cannot stand in the way of Sino-Indian rapprochement. In her recent speeches abroad Indira Gandhi made it clear that she was opposed to Big Power hegemony.

There is a wide body of opinion who are concerned about the five-fold increase in the defence budget of India since 1962, which has been a continuing cause of the spiralling inflation in our country. They would welcome any serious effort for a Sino-Indian detenté, which may be taken up to-day by our Government.

Another factor which made quiet diplomatic overtures from either side impossible was the unusual decision taken by Nehru in September 1959 under pressure from an angry Parliament to publish the current official correspondence between India and China. Diplomacy can function successfully only in the twilight. Even the highest apostle of 'open diplomacy', President Woodrow Wilson found, when it came to practice, that open negotiation was totally unworkable. India and China came to a tacit agreement sometime back to stop publication of protest notes in the White Papers.

There is reason to believe that some sort of negotiations have been going on between the Indian and Chinese diplomats in capitals of countries like the U.A.R. and Rumania. The West Asian correspondent of a leading Indian daily in February 1973 gave us the following conditions raised by China for normalisation of Sino-Indian relations : (1) India must recognise the Aksai Chin region as an integral part of China, (2) the two countries should reach an agreement on a new delineation of frontiers replacing the McMahon Line, (3) withdrawal of Indian support for Tibetan emigrants, which would mean the expulsion of the Dalai Lama and other leaders of the Tibetan nationalist movement, (4) India should stop military intervention in Bangladesh, (5) India should declare that her treaty of friendship with the USSR does not contain any secret clause. In spite of denial by the External Affairs Ministry, there is reason to believe that the above points might have been raised by the Chinese diplomats in negotiations with their Indian counterparts.

We know that on three occasions there have been bilateral negotiations between India and China. In April 1960 when Chou En-lai visited New Delhi, he raised the first three points. When the Secretary-General, Indian External Affairs Ministry Mr R. K. Nehru, visited Peking in July 1961, he was told that China would give up their larger claims and would recognise India's sovereignty over Kashmir in return for India's acceptance of her sovereignty over Aksai Chin. When Krishna Menon and China's Foreign Minister Chen Yi met in Geneva in July 1962, there were further talks. According to Kuldip Nayar, "Menon had told Chen Yi.... that India might accept China's suzerainty over the area in Aksai Chin.... In exchange China must officially accept the McMahon Line and India's right to the rest of Ladakh". (*Between The Lines,* p. 136). The new conditions raised by China relating to withdrawal of the Indian Army from Bangladesh has practically no relevance to-day. The delay in the repatriation of Pakistani prisoners of war was caused mainly by the Pakistani intransigence about the repatriation of Bengali civil population. China was one of the 104 member-states of the U.N., who passed a resolution in the General Assembly in October 1972 urging immediate repatriation of the Pakistani P.O.W's. China has also delayed the recognition of Bangladesh and vetoed her entry into the United Nations. It was, however, hoped that the Pakistani P.O.W. question would be settled in the near future along with related problems, and both Pakistan and China would extend recognition to Bangladesh. Sino-Indian irritations over the break-up of Pakistan and creation of Bangladesh are not expected to last long.

It will not be difficult for India to assure China that there are no secret military clauses in the Sino-Soviet Treaty aimed against China. India in any circumstances is not going to pull chestnuts out of the fire for the sake of others.

So the prospects of a Sino-Indian detenté will depend largely on how India can tackle the three old points of dispute. K. P. S. Menon, who was largely responsible for building up the Indo-Soviet relations into a mighty structure from a rather weak foundation during the years 1952-1961, (he also held such key offices as Foreign Secretary during 1948-1952, and was the first Indian Ambassador in China) lamented in his memoirs that India lost a good chance in improving relations with China in April 1960 on a reasonable basis. Under Chou En-lai's proposal, the Chinese Government would recognize the McMahon Line once and for all in return for some recognition on our part of Chinese claims to the disputed Aksai Chin area. "Nehru seemed personally disposed to negotiate on the frontier problem, but he gave up the idea and assumed an inflexible posture as a result of the opposition of some of his senior colleagues in the Cabinet and criticism in Parliament". (*Twilight in China*, p. 260). It should be noted that K. P. S. Menon was the first Indian to hold a responsible position in the Foreign and Political Department of the Government of India under the British Raj, and he knew better than anybody else that we did not inherit a firm legal claim to the McMahon Line, though geographically it should be an acceptable claim line. Many people forget that before July 1954, the Survey of India maps showed the northern frontier in the Aksai Chin area as 'Undefined'.

We may conclude this study in an optimistic note with a quotation from Shakespeare :

"There is a tide in the affairs of men,
   Which, taken at the flood, leads on to fortune,

SINO-INDIAN RELATIONS—THE PROSPECTS OF A DETENTÉ 61

Omitted, all the voyage of their life
Is bound in shallows and miseries".

There is also a tide in the affairs of nations and at present the tide is in favour of a reconciliation between two great Asian nations—India and China, as it is also in favour of detenté between the Great Powers. In China, the militarists from General Lin Piao downwards have suffered an eclipse. And next only to Mao Tse-tung, Chou En-lai, acutest of politicians and diplomats, has emerged as the most influential figure in China. In India, Prime Minister Indira Gandhi still holds an unchallenged position in the ruling party, in the Cabinet and in Parliament. So she is in a better position than her father to take a bold initiative to end the period of rancour and bitterness with China. Establishment of good-neighbourly relations with China will open new vistas for Indian diplomacy as an eloquent advocate of the cause of the Third World.

THE McMAHON LINE : FROM A MYTH TOWARDS REALITY

The McMahon Line has been widely regarded as a definitive boundary depicting the North-Eastern frontier of India. This Line is supposed to be a product of the Tri-partite Simla Conference of 1913-14 in which Britain, China and Tibet participated. But the documents, available in the India Office Library, show that this Line was agreed to by the British Plenipotentiary Sir Henry McMahon and the Tibetan Plenipotentiary through a secret exchange of Notes, dated 24th and 25th March, 1914, without the participation of the Chinese Plenipotentiary. The British Indian Government did not regard this Line as legally valid, primarily because of the prohibitive clauses of the Anglo-Russian Convention (1907).* Lord Hardinge, the Governor-General of India, in a Note to the Secretary of State for India on 23rd July, 1914, made it clear that the consideration of the North Eastern Frontier of India was not a part of the functions of the Simla Conference and that the views and proposals, put forward by Sir Henry McMahon in this respect, might be regarded as only personal, having no endorsement of the Government of India.

In the Volume XIV of *Aitchison's Treaties* (1929 edition) published under the authority of the Foreign and Political Department, Government of India, it was said, "In 1913 a conference of Tibetan, Chinese and British Plenipotentiaries met in India to try and bring about a settlement in regard to matters on the Sino-Tibetan Frontier; and a tri-partite Convention was drawn up and initialled in 1914. The Chinese Government, however, refused to permit their Plenipotentiary to proceed to full signature". The Volume XIV of the 1929 edition of *Aitchison's Treaties* was, however, withdrawn from circulation by the Government of India and surreptitiously replaced by a spurious edition printed in 1938 with an imprint of 1929. In this new version of the Volume XIV

---

* The Anglo-Russian Convention says, "In conformity with the admitted principle of the suzerainty of China over Tibet, Great Britain and Russia engage not to enter into negotiations with Tibet except through the intermediary of the Chinese Government."

of *Aitchison's Treaties,* it was said that the Simla Conference convened in 1913 was to negotiate an agreement as to the international status of Tibet with particular regard to the relations of Britain, China and Tibet and to the frontier of Tibet both with China and India. It referred to the refusal by the Chinese Government to ratify the Convention but asserted that the Simla Convention was ratified by Great Britain and Tibet by means of a declaration accepting the terms as binding between themselves.

This surreptious alteration of the narrative about the Simla Convention was done mainly on the initiative of Sir Olaf Caroe and this has been a continuing source of confusion in free India about the true legacy of the British Raj in regard to the North Eastern Frontier.

II

From the geographic point of view, however, the McMahon Line may rightly be regarded as a natural border between India and China, as it represents, approximately, the crest line of the Himalayas. And the Indian External Affairs Ministry, under the able guidance of its first Foreign Secretary K. P. S. Menon, made vigorous efforts to push the administrative centres in the NEFA area south of the McMahon Line. Though the Chinese maps since the early thirties had consistently showed the boundary in this region along the foothills of Assam, the Chinese Government had no direct claim to any part of the NEFA area. Also by virtue of their suzerainty over Tibet, they could advance their claim only to Walong and the Tawang tract in this region. According to Dr Alastair Lamb, "Apart from its inclusion within India of Tawang and Walong, the McMahon Line conflicted surprisingly little with Tibetan concepts as to their sphere of influence". (*The China-India Border,* page 151). Tawang was a part of the Tsona district in Tibet and hundreds of monks in its great monastery were closely connected to the Drepung monastery in Lhasa, which was a major force in Tibetan politics. On the other hand, the Tawang region was of special strategic importance to India, lying along the eastern boundary of Bhutan. The Government of India under the British Raj had taken Walong in 1943. But they gave up the project of pushing administration upto the McMahon Line in the Tawang tract in the face of Tibetan opposition, because it would be incompatible with their overall objective of drawing Tibet into the British sphere of influence and bolstering up Tibet as a friendly buffer-state against China. But after independence, because of the change of power realities in Asia, the Government of India under Nehru came to the conclusion that "the British Policy (which we were supposed to have inherited) of looking upon Tibet as area in which we have special political interests could not be maintained" (K. M. Panikkar: *In Two Chinas*, Page 102). So unlike the British, free India was in a better position to take over the Tawang tract by a show of force from the Tibetan Government, provided such action did not lead to the Chinese intervention in the matter. It is to the credit of the External Affairs Ministry, then under the Secretaryship of K. P. S. Menon, that the Indian occupation of Tawang was planned in January-February, 1951, at a time when China was locked in grim battle in Korea with the American forces under the U.N. flag, and there was a complete deadlock in Sino-Tibetan relations. Because of India's friendly attitude towards the People's Republic of China in regard to her claim to occupy the seat of China in the Security Council as a permanent member in preference to the Taiwan Government, as also India's recognition of the vital interest of China in the security of North Korea, together with India's disavowal of political interests in Tibet, created an atmosphere of understanding between India and China at that period. And so India was able to accomplish the incorporation of the Tawang tract, which was of strategic importance to her, without a murmur from the Government of China in 1951. It was a remarkable fact that there were no protests since January, 1950, upto the Tibetan uprising in March, 1959, about the steady advance of Indian administration above the foothills of Assam by the People's Republic of China, in contrast to the intransigent attitude of the Nationalist Government of China who submitted several protest Notes during 1946-1949 on the issue. In a telegram dated 16th October, 1947, the Tibetan Government also made tall territorial claims upon the Government of India.

According to the minute of Nehru-Chou conversations held during the visit of the Chinese Prime Minister to India in the winter of 1956-1957, as maintained by Nehru, we find the following comments made by Chou En-lai on the McMahon Line :

"Although he thought that this line, established by British Imperialism, was not fair, nevertheless, (1) because it was an accomplished fact and (2) because of the friendly relations which existed between China and the countries concerned namely, India and Burma, the Chinese Government were of the opinion that they should give recognition to the McMahon Line. (3) They had, however, not consulted the Tibetan authorities about it yet. They proposed to do so." (*White Paper* No. 1, Page 50).

Conflict between India and China over the control of some perepheral areas along the McMahon Line first arose in 1959 in the wake of the Tibetan revolt, which soured India-China relations. According to the opinion of the Surveyor-General of India (as given in his confidential Note to the Foreign Secretary, dated 23rd March, 1937), there were inaccuracies and uncertainties in the original map of the McMahon Line in the Thagla Ridge sector and the Subansiri region about Longju, where the first India-China clash occurred in August, 1959. Anyway, if the Indian border claims were limited to the Chinese recognition of the McMahon Line, it would not have resulted in an imbroglio causing a costly confrontation along the whole stretch of the extensive Northern border from Ladakh to NEFA for the last fifteen years. China's military withdrawal after the border invasion in October, 1962, in the NEFA region and her acquiscence to the re-establishment of Indian administration in this area on a firmer footing in recent years (as Arunachal Pradesh) also indicate China's agreeableness to accept the *fait accompli* of the McMahon Line (provided that her claim in the Aksai Chin area is accepted by India).

THE NORTH-EAST FRONTIER OF INDIA : THE BRITISH LEGACY

On 13th August, 1959, Prime Minister Nehru said, "So far as we are concerned, the McMahon Line is the firm frontier by treaty, firm by usage, firm by geography". On the other hand, we have the testimony of Sir Henry Twynum, the Acting Governor of Assam in 1939, who in a letter to The Times of 2nd September, 1959, stated : "The McMahon Line, which sought to secure the main crest of the Himalayas as the frontier, does not exist and never has existed". Thus the confusion about the legal position of India's North-East frontier still continues.

In a speech on 30th June, 1959, at the East India Association, London, H. E. Richardson, who was head of the British and later the Indian Mission in Lhasa for several years, referred to recent developments in Tibet and the danger to India's frontiers, which had apparently been highlighted by Sir Olaf Caroe thus,—"Sir Olaf Caroe knows a great deal about the problem. In 1936 he discovered that the exact position and nature of India's frontier with Tibet was more or less unknown. By an agreement called the McMahon Line, reached in 1914, it runs roughly along the main axis of the Himalayas. And it was due to Sir Olaf that the frontier was revived and was made very much a reality; and what he started has been kept up." (*Asian Review*: October 1959).

On 21 October, 1959, it was Sir Olaf Caroe's turn to address the East India Association, his subject being THE INDIA-TIBET-CHINA TRIANGLE. In reply to a query about the North-East Frontier of India, he said : "The McMahon Line was drawn just before World War I and then forgotten, and actually I know all about this because I was Deputy Secretary in the Foreign Department in 1936 and it was I who discovered that it had been forgotten. The Times Atlases and all the rest of them were showing the frontier of India as running along here (along the foothills) while by treaty it was up there (along the crest line). So when I came on leave, I went along to various authorities, including The Times, whom I did not manage to interest very much more then than one can now in this matter, and pointed out that about 400 miles of India had been shown as inside Tibet and potentially inside China. It was World War I, the preoccupations of World War I, which led to this line being forgotten and left on the files". (*Asian Review* : January 1960).

Sir Olaf Caroe's claim about the 'discovery' of the McMahon Line after a lapse of more than twenty years is corroborated by K. P. S. Menon, who was a former colleague of his in the Foreign Department and later became the Foreign Secretary to the Government of India during 1948-52. Menon writes in his autobiography, *Many Worlds,* "In 1913-14 took place a tripartite conference between Great Britain, China and Tibet when the frontier between India, China and Tibet was defined, and the famous McMahon Line came into existence. The Chinese, however, refused to ratify this agreement. Thereafter, for over 30 years, the Government of India simply took the McMahon Line for granted; they could afford to do so because China, torn by civil wars, was in no position to assert herself, and the Tibet, under a strong Dalai Lama, was firmly addicted to its independence. Caroe, however, with a prescience which, in the light of the events of the sixties must be regarded as remarkable, realized that the north-east frontier might one day become as live as the north-west, and pressed for the rudiments of administration, civil and military, into areas abutting the McMahon Line. But for his foresight independent India might have found herself in an even more difficult position to resist the Chinese advance". (pp. 139-140).

On perusal of the documents available in the India Office Library, however, we find that in fixing the McMahon Line—which had been secretly agreed upon between the British and the Tibetan delegates (on 24/25th March, 1914), and was later (on 27th April, 1914) presented as an extension of the Red Line depicting the proposed boundary between China and Inner Tibet in the Simla Convention map—Sir Henry McMahon went beyond the instructions of the British Government. On 23rd July, 1914, the Viceroy Lord Hardinge, in forwarding a copy of the Final Memorandum of Sir Henry, the British Plenipotentiary, Tibet Conference, to the Secretary of State, London wrote *inter alia;* ".... we recognise that a consideration of the eastern or Indo-Chinese portion of the North-East Frontier did not form part of the functions of the Conference...." (Memo B 206) [*India Office Records* : Pol. 464: Pts. 5 & 6: L/P & S/10/344. *Political and Secret Memo* B 206. No. 90 of 1914 G.O.I. Foreign and Political Department. Hardinge to Crew, 23 July, 1914]. In Volume XIV of the *Aitchison's Treaties* published in 1929, the following reference was made to the Simla Convention (no mention being made of the McMahon Line) : "In 1913 a conference of Tibetan, Chinese and British Plenipotentiaries met in India to try and bring about a settlement with regard to matters on the Sino-Tibetan Frontier: and a tri-partite Convention was drawn up and initialled in 1914. The Chinese Government, however, refused to permit their Plenipotentiary to proceed to full signature."

From the correspondence between the Government of Assam and F. Williamson, who was then (i.e. during 1934-35) the Political Officer of Sikkim, over the location of the eastern boundary of Bhutan, it appears that there was some confusion as to whether the semi-independent tribes living in the triangle south of the Se La range were within the political influence of Tibet or Assam itself. ("The Monba living north of the Sela range are under Tibetan administration". *Aitchison's Treaties* Vol. XII) Williamson admitted in his letter to the Chief Secretary, Assam, (No. 6-(3)-P/35) dated Gangtok, 10th June, 1935 [I.O.R. : Pol. (External) Dept : *Collection* 36/ File 23. P.Z. 5803/1936], that until recent correspondence, he and his predecessors had thought that the location of the eastern boundary was to be settled between Bhutan and Tibet.

In 1935, the well-known British explorer and Botanist Captain Kingdom-Ward made an illegal entry into Tibet from the Assam side and was arrested by the Tibetan authorities. The Tibetan Government protested to Williamson, who was then on a visit to Lhasa. As a result, a new correspondence started between the officials of the Government of India focussing interest on the North-East Frontier beginning with a telegram from the Political Officer, Sikkim, to the Secretary, Political Department, Simla, dated 28th September, 1935 [I.O.R. : Pol. (External) Dept. : *Collection* 37/2 File 28, P.Z. 7569/1935]. On enquiry, it came out that Captain Kingdom-Ward had received verbal permission to enter Tibet from one of the Dzongpons of Tawangdzong. On 5th November, 1935, the Foreign and Political Department sent an identical telegram to the Political Officer, Sikkim, and the Government of Assam in which they said that in connection with the recent boundary dispute between Bhutan and Assam the question of the international frontier between India and Eastern Tibet and Bhutan had been examined by the Government of India. It was asserted in this telegram that the boundary "was defined by Red Line on map drawn by McMahon and accepted by Tibetan Government in accordance with Article IX of 1914 Convention". Since this Line was well north of Tawang, the Government of India made the following queries: "(1) why did Tibetans maintain Dzongpons at Tawang who granted authority to enter Tibet? (2) Are you sure that Kingdon-Ward actually went or is alleged by Tibetans to have gone to the Tibetan side of the Red Line referred to above or have you any reason to suppose that the agreement come to in 1914 has been modified by practice or otherwise since that date?" It was also asserted in the telegram, "It is important that you should not in any way compromise with the Tibetan Government validity of international boundary agreed to in 1914". There is reason to believe that Sir Olaf Caroe was the author of this telegram. Caroe built his case for reasserting a claim to the 'McMahon Line' after a lapse of 21 years by the lawyer's device of presenting a leading question to the Tibetan Government in which reference was made to the Red Line of the Simla Convention as the de facto boundary. [I.O.R. : Pol. (External) Dept. : *Collection* 36/File 29 Telegram No. 3028].

This telegram was answered from Lhasa by Captain Battye, the British Trade Agent who had temporarily succeeded Williamson. Captain Battye's telegram, dated 14th November, 1935, stated: "Tibetan Government allege that Kingdom-Ward went far beyond the Red Line even to Kongbo, Pome and Poyul north of Tsangpo. They maintain that Red Line has not been modified. They say that it will be no use Kingdom-Ward applying for permission to visit Tibet in future and only passports from Tibetan Government are ever valid. Kingdom-Ward has been sent back to India and Tibetan Government are willing to regard incident as closed". [I.O.R. : Pol. (External) Dept. : *Collection* 36/File 29. Telegram R No. 5].

The Chief Secretary, Government of Assam, wrote to the Foreign Secretary, Government of India, on 13th November, 1935:

".... 2. As regards the connection of Tawang with Tibet, The Governor-in-Council believes that Tawang is more or less independent territory, but owes some indirect allegiance to Tibet. The position is partly explained at page 11 of Volume XII of Aitchison's Treaties. It may be that owing to this indirect connection with Tibet the Dzongpons of Tawang considered that they had an authority to grant Kingdom-Ward permission to enter Tibet. So far as information goes there has been no change in recent years in the attitude of the Tibetan Government in respect of their part of the Frontier." [I.O.R. : Pol. (External) Dept. : *Collection* 37/File 28 No. P.Z. 9019/1935].

Caroe wrote another letter to Captain Battye at Lhasa on 28th November, 1935, arguing in favour of a policy of recognising the McMahon Line as the definitive boundary. He referred to the late Williamson's letter of 10th June, 1935, in which "he was apprehensive of a claim by Tibet to the area in the foothills .... and his recommendation is apparently coloured by the thought that it might be expedient to cede to Bhutan, whose foreign relations we control, an area in these hills before Tibet, less controllable neighbour, can present an effective claim". Caroe then asserted in paragraph 2 of his letter, "But the position as regards the international frontier in this region would surely admit of no such claim. Under Article 9 of the 1914 convention, the frontier between Tibet and India was clearly defined, and left to India the entire Tawang area of the hill country east of Bhutan, which includes the strip now proposed for cession to Bhutan. Indeed the agreement then reached carries India's frontier right up into the heart of the Himalayas to a line at least 60 miles north of the area now under discussion." Caroe added, "This particular boundary appears to have been closely defined before the actual conclusion of the Convention, (see Sir Henry McMahon's memorandum dated 28th March, 1914, with enclosures and map attached). Reference should also be made to Sir Henry McMahon's note dated 8th July, 1914, part IV (4), from which it is clear that the whole of the Tawang Hill area in this region north of Assam proper as defined in the map cited was then included in British territory, and is therefore part of India. The actual boundary laid down was marked red in the map which was sent to the Tibetan Government and accepted by them in the exchange of Notes between the British and the Tibetan Plenipotentiaries dated the 24th and 25th March, 1914, as referred to in the first memorandum above."

On the basis of Captain Battye's previous statement in his telegram dated 14th November, 1935, Olaf Caroe said in the above letter : "Incidentally in connection with Kingdon-Ward's case, the Tibetan Government have just re-affirmed this line and say it has not been modified. It appears therefore that Tibet could not in any case put forward a claim to sovereignty over any territory in the foothills east of Bhutan. It seems, therefore, unnecessary that the present issue should be clouded by any fear of presentation or acceptance of such a claim in this region on behalf of Tibet...." [I.O.R. : Pol. (External) Dept. : *Collection* 36/File 23. No. P. Z. 2661/1936].

Caroe sent a copy of the above letter to the Chief Secretary, Assam Government, with a covering D.O. letter dated 28th November, 1935 : ". . . It appears that there has been considerable misunderstanding regarding the international frontier between India and Tibet, as delimited by Sir Henry McMahon in 1914, and accepted by the Tibetan Government. The Government of India will be glad to learn whether this letter is a correct representation of the position as regards the frontier between Assam tribal areas and Tibet."

The Chief Secretary, Assam Government, in his reply on 7th December, 1935, stated that "the Assam Government accept, as correctly stated, the position explained in your secret semi-official letter to Captain Battye . . . We have always in these late years taken the McMahon Line to be Tibet boundary and we are not aware of any claim to the area south of that line since 1914." [I.O.R. Pol. (External) Dept. *Collection* 36/File 23. Assam Secretariat, D.O. No. Pol. 1887/9/85 A.P. This appears to be the first occasion on which the Himalayan crest-line alignment was called the McMahon Line]. This is contrary to fact, as the Survey of India maps upto 1936 showed the boundary along the foothills of Assam. Captain Battye writing to Caroe on 13th December, 1935, said "I agree with you that so far as Tibet is concerned there appears to be no cause for concern at all . . . [I.O.R. : Pol. (External) Dept : *Collection* 36/ File 23. The Residency, Gangtok, Sikkim, D.O. No. 6(3)-P/35]. This was obviously an irresponsible remark by a junior officer, which was contradicted by Basil Gould, Political Officer, Sikkim, in his Telegram XX No. 205 dated 12 December, 1936, Lhasa.

On 6th February, 1936, Caroe wrote identical letters to the Chief Secretary, Assam, and the new Political Officer, Sikkim, enquiring "whether any measure of political control has been extended up to that line in the course of the last twenty years, and in particular whether the Tibetan Government honour the frontier by refraining from administrative measures such as the collection of revenue on the Indian side of the frontier, more specially in the Tawang area." In the same letter, Caroe also emphasised that the external frontier had not been correctly shown on the maps of the Survey of India. [I.O.R. : Pol. (External) Dept. : *Collection* 36/ File 23 : Confidential F.O. No. F. 493-X/135].

On 9th April, 1936, Caroe wrote a personal letter to J.C.E. Walton, Secretary, Political Department, India Office, London, with a view to winning the support of the Secretary of State for India in activating the McMahon Line. The letter ran thus : "..... Indo-Tibetan frontier from the eastern frontier of Bhutan to the Isu Razi Pass on the Irawaddy-Salween water-parting ....was clearly defined under Article IX of the 1914 Convention .... it was in that year decided not to publish Anglo-Tibetan Trade Regulations of 1914 which was made under the 1914 Convention. Similarly the 1914 Convention itself, with McMahon's supplementary boundary agreement with the Tibetan Government .. remained unpublished, and none of these papers appear in Aitchison's Treaties, Volume XII and Volume XIV .... As a result of this restraint when in 1935 the question of location of the frontier of India in the region came up for consideration, it was discovered that both Assam Government and the Political Officer, Sikkim, were ignorant of the position of the frontier. Williamson himself thought that in the Assam sector the International frontier ran along the foothills and was identical with the frontier of the administered districts of the Province of Assam." Caroe then continued : ".... it was only with considerable difficulty and almost by chance that we were able to unearth the true position .. we came to know incidentally from a reference in the Kingdom-Ward case that the McMahon Line .... is well-known to the Tibetan Government, and is still fully accepted by them."* He then argued, ". . . there is a real danger that important matters of this kind may go wrong if we refrain any longer from publishing our agreements with Tibet. ....Their absence from such a publication as Aitchison's Treaties, if it became known to the Chinese Government, might well be used by them in support of the argument that no ratified argument between India and Tibet is in existence. Further reasons for re-affirming our engagement with Tibet on this frontier are supplied by the necessity of defining in connection with the New Constitution the tribal areas on the north-east, which it is proposed will be under the political control of the Governor of Assam...." In addition to stressing the necessity of inserting in *Aitchison's Treaties* the text of the 1914 Anglo-Tibetan Convention together with the exchange of notes regarding the boundary and the Trade Regulations made under the Convention, Caroe urged that "steps should be taken without delay to show this boundary on the maps of the Survey of India." [I.O.R. : Pol. (External) Dept. : *Collection* 36/ File 23, No. P.Z. 2788/1936].

In a letter to Caroe dated 16th July, [I.O.R. : Pol. (External) Dept. : *Collection* 36/ File 23, No. P.Z. 4911/36], J. C. Walton from the India Office informed him of the approval of the Secretary of State for India, regarding the Government of India's proposals, subject to the following points : (a) Whether or not the Government of India contemplated a re-issue of Volume XIV of *Aitchison's Treaties* in the immediate future; the Survey of India maps could show the frontier; (b) When the agreements are published it would be most desirable to avoid unnecessary publicity and to refrain from drawing the attention of the press or news agencies to the publication. (c) ..It would be desirable not to publish the text of the Declaration of 3rd July, 1914, by the Plenipotentiaries of Great Britain and Tibet, accepting the Simla Convention as binding on their two Governments, but to deal with it merely by means of a Note to be inserted in *Aitchison* (to the effect that whereas the Simla Convention itself after being initialled by the Chinese Plenipotentiary was not signed or ratified by the Chinese Government, it was

---

*This was at best a half-truth, which was contradicted by Basil Gould in his telegram from Lhasa, dated 12th December, 1936.

accepted as binding by the two other parties as between themselves).

Thus receiving the permission from the Secretary of State, the Government of India immediately proceeded in the matter of producing a revised version of *Aitchison* and Survey of India maps. Also in a letter dated 17th August, 1936, the Government of India proposed to the India Office that Basil Gould (the new Political Officer, Sikkim), who would shortly be visiting Lhasa, should raise the matter of Tibetan administrative control and the collection of revenues for purely civil purposes in the Tawang area. It was also suggested that he obtained from the Tibetan Government a written re-affirmation of the 1914 frontier. A further suggestion that a protest be made to the Chinese Government about cartographical encroachments in the North East Frontier of India was put forward. [I.O.R. : Pol. (External) Dept. : *Collection* 36/File 23 No. P.Z. 6153/1936].

The India Office, London, in their telegram of 16th September, 1936, [I.O.R. : Pol. (External) Dept. : *Collection* 36/File 23 P.Z. 6153/36] approved the first two proposals. But on the issue of making a protest to the Chinese Government against the usurpation of Indian territory on Chinese maps, the India Office as well as the Foreign Office maintained their reservations. J. C. Walton wrote to the Secretary, Foreign and Political Department, Government of India, on 15th October, 1936, [I.O.R. : Pol. (External) Dept : *Collection* 36/File 23 P.Z. 6154/36] ". . . such a protest should not be made, as it would be likely to lead to undesirable discussion with the Chinese Government regarding the validity of the 1914 Agreements, and possibly to an increased Chinese interest in the tribal territories on the northern border of Assam . . . . they could . . . quote the manner in which the boundary is shown on British maps, including the map printed in the present edition of the India Office List . . ."

NEGOTIATIONS AT LHASA

Basil Gould had been carrying on negotiations with the Kashag (Tibetan Cabinet) since his arrival at Lhasa in September 1936. There were various urgent political issues arising out of the presence at Lhasa of a Chinese Diplomatic Mission led by General Huang-Mu-Sung, the possibility of a reconciliation between the Panchen Lama and the Kashag, and the question of military support to Tibet against any possible danger from China. When Gould raised the question of Tawang and the McMahon Line, the Kashag replied: ". . . (1) upto 1914 Tawang had undoubtedly been Tibetan, (2) they regarded the adjustment of the Tibet-Indian boundary as part and parcel of the general adjustment and determination of boundaries contemplated in the 1914 Convention. If they could with our (British) help, secure a definitive Sino-Tibetan boundary they would of course be glad to observe the Indo-Tibetan boundary as defined in 1914, (3) they have been encouraged in thinking that His Majesty's Government and the Government of India sympathised with this way of regarding the matter owing to the fact that at no time since the Convention and Declaration of 1914 had the Indian Government taken steps to question Tibetan, or assert British, authority in the Tawang area." [I.O.R. : Pol. (External) Dept. : *Collection* 36/File 29 No. P.Z. 3850/1936].

The Foreign and Political Department sent a telegram to Basil Gould on 8th December, 1936 [I.O.R. : Pol. (External) Dept. : *Collection* 36/File 29; Telegram XX No. 2929, 8 December, 1936, New Delhi] as follows : "Tawang. Attitude of Kashag is wholly untenable . . . you should point out that Indo-Tibetan frontier was separately agreed to by exchange of Notes 24th and 25th March, 1914. Moreover, Tibetan Government indicated adherence to McMahon Line in connection with Kingdon-Ward case as recently as November, 1935 . . . On neither occasion was there any suggestion that Tibetan Government's observance of McMahon Line was dependent on securing definite Sino-Tibetan boundary."

Basil Gould replied, [I.O.R. : Pol. (External) Dept. : *Collection* 363/File 29; Telegram XX No. 205, 12 December 1936, Lhasa].: ". . . It appears on close examination that it is improbable that Kashag made any useful admission on the occasion of interview with Battye on Kingdon-Ward case.

"I apprehend if at present stage I were to suggest written reaffirmation, my action would tend to create impression that we ourselves feel that engagement of 1914 stand in need of reaffirmation; and it is practically certain that Tibetan Government would decline to reaffirm especially in writing except after reference to Regent, Prime Minister, National Assembly and Monasteries, who were signatories to Declaration of 3rd July, 1914. China would in one way or another be likely to make capital out of such requirements and opportunity would be given to Tibetan Government to attempt to attach to negotiations for reaffirmations all sorts of request vis-a-vis China."

Basil Gould favoured definite action in Tawang, backed by reiteration of oral explanation in Lhasa rather than raising the question of reaffirmation. He further suggested collecting of more information about the little known North-East border region in which it was intended gradually to assert authority and more personal contact between the Political Officer, Sikkim, and the Assam Government.

OLAF CAROE TRIES TO MOVE THE INDIA OFFICE

Olaf Caroe went to England on Home leave in February 1937. There is some evidence to suggest that he sought to persuade the India Office and the Foreign Office, (hitherto bothered only about the Russian bogey along the North-West frontier) of the possible dangers arising from present or future Chinese moves on the North-East frontier. This prodding by Caroe moved R. A. Butler, Parliamentary Under-Secretary of State for India, to seek information from J. C. Walton, the Secretary, Political Department, India Office. On 13th March, 1937, Walton wrote to Butler : "The Simla Convention of 1914, which lay down the true frontier between India and Tibet, including that part of the latter which is now claimed by China, were not published on account (at the time) of complication arising from the Anglo-Russian Convention of 1907, and subsequently in order to avoid stimulating Chinese interest in Tibet. These reasons have now ceased to be valid, and it was decided last autumn to publish them in a revised edition of Vol. XIV of *Aitchison's Treaties* to be brought out specially for the purpose. The true frontier is also to be shown on map published by the Survey of India. Since Mr Caroe spoke to me on this subject, we have asked the Government of India to send either direct or through the India Office copies of the new Survey of India maps to the leading firms of cartographers in this country and draw their attention to the point. The Royal Geographical Society and War Office will also be informed. The map in the India Office List has already been corrected in this year's edition." [I.O.R. : Pol. (External) Dept. : *Collection* 36 (2)/File 23].

The Secretary of State for India sent a telegram on 1st April 1937 to the Government of India enquiring about the results of the Gould Mission to Tibet. The Foreign and Political Department replied on 19th April, 1937 [I.O.R. : Pol. (External) Dept. : *Collection* 36/File 23 No. P.Z. 2644/1937] : ".... Gould does not think that Tibetan Government are contemplating any immediate action ... We, therefore, recommend that Richardson (Officer-in-charge of the British Mission in Lhasa) should be instructed to take no action unless Tibetan Government again refer to proposal (for bi-partite negotiations with China mainly on the question of the return of the Panchen Lama to Tibet with Chinese armed escorts) and ask for advice or facilities for emissaries to travel through India. Although His Majesty's Government have no objection for despatch of Tibetan emissary to open preliminary and informal discussions, they would like to be represented at any general negotiations which might affect their Treaty rights vis-a-vis Tibet or Tibet's own status as an autonomous state under the suzerainty of China..."

VIEWS OF THE ASSAM GOVERNMENT ON THE TAWANG ISSUE

The views of the Governor of Assam (who was ex-officio Agent to the Governor-General regarding the tribal areas on the North-East frontier) were forwarded to the Government of India in Assam letter of 27th May, 1937. This letter recalled that in 1914 Sir Henry McMahon had urged that a tactful and discreet officer be posted to Tawang for the summer months, with instructions to collect a light tax but at the same time to leave the people to manage their own affairs. "His Excellency considers that the time has now come when the policy advocated in 1914 but so long held in abeyance should be carried out." [Sir Robert Reid, *History of the Frontier Areas Bordering on Assam* (Shillong : The Assam Government Press, 1942) pp. 294-297].

After further consideration, it was proposed that, as a preliminary, a small expedition would go to Tawang, "examine the country, get into touch with the inhabitants, and form some estimate of its revenue possibilities" before a final decision was reached. This was agreed to by the Government of India.

THE LEAGUE OF NATIONS SLAVERY CONVENTION : ITS IMPACT ON BRITISH POLICY TOWARDS TRIBAL AREAS BORDERING ON ASSAM

The Slavery Committee urged the members of the League of Nations to suppress the practice of slavery in all areas within their territorial jurisdiction and report to them on the matter. But the Government of India made reservation about their acceptance of the Slavery Convention with regard to the unadministered area of the Sadiya and Balipara frontier tracts. In their letter to the Secretary of State dated 20th August, 1936, (No. F. 66-X/35), the Government of India said, "..... complete abolition of slavery in all its forms would necessitate the actual occupation of the country and the establishment of regular administration, a course which would be quite impracticable as the country is inaccessible for the greater part of the year and is inhabited by intractable population." This information was sent to the League Slavery Committee by the Secretary of State for India in September 1936. The League Advisory Committee on Slavery in paragraph 17 of their Report of 10th April 1937 compared maintenance of reservation in respect of Sadiya and Balipara tracts, on ground that they were unadministered, with unreserved acceptance of the Convention by European Powers in respect to their colonies, some areas in which might be even more remote.

The Secretary of State for India in a telegram to the External Affairs Department, Government of India, on 26th July, 1937, [I.O.R. : Pol. (External) Dept. : *Collection* 36/File 23 E & O 4284/37], referred to the above report and said, "Admission made in reservation that areas are unadministered might be used to support the Chinese claims, and from this point of view it is desirable to avoid the further advertisement of lack of control which is involved in the maintenance of reservation and its defence in Geneva." He further advised, "There would be advantage in announcing withdrawal during the next League Assembly which opens on 13th September."

On 16th February, 1938, the following communication was sent to the Secretary-General, League of Nations, ".... the Government of India has once again reviewed the reservation appended to the Indian signature of the Slavery Commission of 1936 in respect of 'the unadministered parts of Sadiya and Balipara Frontier Tracts,' and in view of the comments of the Committee, has decided to withdraw the reservation. Preliminary steps are being taken with a view to extending the necessary control in these areas." [I.O.R. : Pol. (External) Dept. : *Collection* 36/File 23 E & O 944/38].

British Expedition to Tawang in April, 1938

Captain Lightfoot, with his retinue of the Assam Rifles and a few hundred porters arrived at Tawang on 30 April 1938. Their arrival soon came to the ears of the Tibetan Government, who protested to B. J. Gould, the Political Officer in Sikkim, and asked that the expedition should be withdrawn. Meanwhile, Captain Lightfoot had reported on the 26th April that the Tibetan officials had been collecting taxes in presence of the expedition and asked that they may be made to withdraw. The Governor of Assam also wanted that the Tibetan Government should be requested to withdraw their officials to their side of the international boundary. The Government of India, however, were averse to any action which would commit them to permanent occupation and further expenditure. They intimated that "Lightfoot should inform all concerned that Tawang was by treaty Indian and not Tibetan territory and should impress this on Tibetan officials if he meets them. He should not, however, demand their withdrawal and should give no assurance to local inhabitants but should simply inform them that he has been sent to make enquiries into local conditions and the Government will decide after he returns whether to take any further interest in them or not." [I.O.R. : Pol. (External) Dept. : *Register* No. P.Z. 3507/38, *Telegram R.* No. 899, 4 May, 1938. From Gould, Yatung to Foreign (Simla). See also Robert Reid, *History of Frontier Areas*, p. 297].

Captain Lightfoot furnished a full and accurate report of conditions as he found in Tawang. He found that the Tawang area itself north of the Sela Pass was completely under Tibetan administration and had been since long before 1914, and that the Tibetan revenue collectors had extended their activities into the Dirang Dzong and Kalaktang areas. The inhabitants of these three areas, which in the case of Tawang were of Bhutanese origin, and in the case of other two areas of tribal origin, were severely oppressed.

Captain Lightfoot concluded his report with the following statement : "The Tibetan Government should be asked to withdraw their officials, viz. the Tsona Dzongpons and their assistants. With them will automatically disappear their exactions of tribute and forced labour. Till this is done our prestige must inevitably be non-existent." He recommended the loose administration of the area by British Officers to the exclusion of the Tibetans. His proposals received support from Sir Robert Reid, the then Governor of Assam. But for financial reasons, the Government of India desisted from sending another expedition to Tawang.

Tibetan Diplomatic Counter-offensive

The Lightfoot expedition led to an adverse reaction in Lhasa. The Tibetan Government called on Rai Bahadur Norbu Dhondup, Assistant to the Political Officer, Sikkim, and said that they had received a joint report from the Tsona Dzongpon and the Tawang Monastery that Captain Lightfoot, with about two hundred troops and six hundred coolies, arrived at Takzong near Tawang and that the expedition desired to come to Tawang. The Tibetan Government enquired why the expedition had come without notifying them and said they would issue orders to stop the expedition coming to Tawang. Rai Bahadur Norbu Dhondup was, however, able to convince the Tibetan Government about the futility of such action. Captain Lightfoot's report from Tawang to the Governor of Assam revealed that the Tibetan Government, on the plea that Tawang area had never been ceded to India, intended to fix their own boundary with the Bhutan Government in that area, with a view to obtaining admission from Bhutan that Tawang was Tibetan. [I.O.R. : Pol. (External) Dept. : *Collection* 36/File 29, *Register No.* P.Z. 5109/1938]. The Government of India was able to check this Tibetan initiative by advising the Political Officer, Sikkim, to inform the Bhutan Government that the Tawang area was British and to request them not to enter into negotiations with the Tibetan Government regarding the boundary between that area and Bhutan. Since by the Treaty of 1910, Bhutan had bound herself to be guided by the Government of India in her foreign relations, this prevented any further complication arising out of Tibetan overtures to Bhutan.

Futile Negotiations at Lhasa : Tibetan Procrastinations

Rai Bahadur Norbu Dhondup had been holding negotiations in Lhasa with the members of the Tibetan Cabinet with a view to inducing them to agree to a voluntary withdrawal of their administration from the Tawang area. In a letter dated 26th August, 1938 [I.O.R. : Pol. (External) Dept. *Collection* 36/File 29, *Confidential letter* No. 3 (5)-L/37, Lhasa, 26 August 1938] to the Political Officer, Sikkim, he related his frustrating experiments in the matter : "... The Kashag told me frankly that they were ashamed of themselves in not being able to fulfil their repeated promises to let me have their decision on the subject. They then explained that most of the officers who had been to India in connection with the Anglo-Tibetan Simla Conference of 1913-14 had expired and some of them had already retired from the Government service and that the present Cabinet Ministers and the King (Regent) are all ignorant of the knowledge that Tawang was ceded to British India. They added that it takes a long while to trace documents on any subject as the office records of the Tibetan Government are not kept in proper order as the offices of other countries do. Moreover, they stated that some of the relevant documents of 1913-14 Simla Treaty are with the Regent and some papers are in other offices, which are not easily traceable. They, therefore, could not go through the question. They also added that office works are carried out very slowly in the offices of the Tibetan Government and that I, therefore, should not take an exception for the delay ....

"2. In the meanwhile, the Kashag asked me to furnish them with a copy of the Treaty clause by virtue of which Tawang was ceded to the British Government. They said that on the receipt of this they will confer among themselves. They, however, made me understand distinctly that the settlement of the question will take time, as they are not empowered to decide such an important question without referring it to the National Assembly.

"3. In accordance with the above discussion, I have sent a copy of Article 9 of the 1914 Convention together with a covering letter...

"4. So far as I have seen the Kashag not less than 9 times and the Regent 3 times about Tawang. All of them are afraid to come to a decision in the matter and the explanation given by them regarding the possible delay in going through the question is merely a pretence. As they said definitely that they want time to come to a decision, I am afraid, it means that the matter will be delayed for many months or years, as they have done in the case of the Tehri-Tibet boundary dispute, which has remained unsettled for so many years...."

PUBLICATION OF REVISED VERSION OF VOLUME XIV OF AITCHISON'S TREATIES

The revised edition of Volume XIV of *Aitchison's Treaties* was produced by the Government of India in August 1938. Sixty-two copies of the revised edition were forwarded to the Under-Secretary, India Office, London, in substitution of those in his possession, along with a request that the old copies be destroyed. (At least two copies of the old version of Volume XIV of the McMahon Line escaped destruction and are still available, one at the Harvard University Library discovered by John Addis, a British diplomat, and another at the India Office Library noticed by the author). This new edition, surreptitiously published in 1938, but carrying the imprint of the 1929 edition, has been a source of endless confusion among the scholars as to the legal status of the Simla Convention Agreements in India and elsewhere. The original 1929 edition of *Aitchison* (Vol. XIV) did not, as we know, publish the text of the Simla Convention, the exchange of the letters of March 24 and 25 between Sir Henry McMahon and Lonchen Shatra about India-Tibet frontier. Also there was no mention about the new Anglo-Tibetan Trade Agreements. In this original version, there was reference to a tripartite conference to "bring about a settlement with regard to matters on *the Sino-Tibetan Frontier*" (p. 21). There was no mention of Indo-Tibetan frontier at all. On the Anglo-Tibetan

Trade Agreements, it merely referred to the fact that modifications in the 1908 Anglo-Tibetan Trade Regulations could not be effective "as a result of the *abortive tri-partite Convention of 1914.*" (p. 20) and admitted that the 1908 Trade Regulations "still remain the basis of the Indo-Tibetan arrangements" (p. 20) (Art. 3 of Tibet Trade Regulations (1908) said, "The administration of the trade marts shall remain with the Tibetan Officers, under the Chinese Officers' supervision.")

In the new surreptitiously published edition of *Aitchison's Treaties*, Vol. XIV (bearing an imprint of 1929, though actually printed in 1938), we get a revised narrative of the 1914 Convention as follows: "In 1913 a conference of British, Chinese and Tibetan Plenipotentiaries was convened in Simla in an attempt to negotiate an agreement as to the international status of Tibet with particular regard to the relations of the three Governments and to the frontier of Tibet both with China and India. After prolonged negotiations, the conference under the presidency of Sir Henry McMahon drew up a tri-partite Convention between Great Britain, China and Tibet, which was initialled in Simla in 1914 by the representatives of the three parties. The Chinese Government, however, refused to ratify the agreements, by their refusal depriving themselves of the benefits which they were to obtain thereunder, among which were a definite recognition that Tibet was under Chinese suzerainty, and an agreement to permit a Chinese official with a suitable escort not exceeding 300 men to be maintained at Lhasa. The Convention was, however, ratified by Great Britain and Tibet by means of a declaration accepting its terms as binding between themselves.

"The Convention included a definition of boundary both on the Sino-Tibetan and the Indo-Tibetan frontier. On the Sino-Tibetan frontier a double boundary was laid down, the portion between the two boundaries being spoken of as Inner Tibet and that part of Tibet lying west of the westerly boundary as Outer Tibet.

"Owing to the failure of the Chinese Government to ratify, these boundaries, however, remained fluid. The other frontier between India and Tibet on the Assam and Burma borders, which has been accepted by His Majesty's Government and the Tibetan Government was laid down between the eastern border of Bhutan and the Isurazi Pass on the Irrawady-Saiween water-parting. West of the Brahmaputra bend, this frontier for the most part follows the main axis of the Himalayas, and east of that point includes all the tribal territory under the political control of Assam and Burma Governments. This frontier throughout stands back some 100 miles from the plains of India and Burma.

"A new set of trade regulations between Great Britain and Tibet were concluded under the Convention to replace the earlier regulations of 1893 and 1908."

THE DRAWING OF THE MCMAHON LINE IN SURVEY OF INDIA MAPS IN 1937

The Surveyor-General of India, who had been asked to show the frontier between India and Tibet, and Bhutan and the Balipara Frontier Tract on the basis of the Red Line in the Simla Convention maps, sent to the Foreign Secretary, Government of India, on 23rd March, 1937, two proofs of the map entitled *"Highlands of Tibet and Surrounding Countries"* on which the McMahon Line was marked. In the covering letter, [I.O.R. : Pol. (External) Dept. : *Collection* 36/File 23, *Confidential letter* No. 865/S, dated 23rd March 1937] he said, ". . . 2. Your attention is drawn to the following points :

"(i) The Red Line indicating the boundary does not follow the watershed at height 21431 (Square C/5), between heights 21488 and 23054 (Square D/5) and near height 15721 (Square E/4). *It has been presumed that these are printed errors and that the boundary should follow the watershed, and it has been shown accordingly on Sheets* 83A *and* 82H.

"(ii) The portion of the boundary where it leaves the watershed south of Photrang (Square E/4) to where it meets the watershed again North-East of Mighitun (Square E/3) has been entered with reference to surrounding detail. *As this portion of the boundary is liable to alteration when the positions of Tso Karpo and Tsari Sarpa are fixed it should, I feel, be marked "approximate" on published maps.* (The village Longju falls in this area—*K.G.*)

"(iii) There is a considerable discrepancy on the common edge of the two sections of the map in your proceedings: the

Red Lines do not coincide. Would you kindly decide on the correct alignment of the boundary here?

"(iv) The more recent surveys show that the ridge north of the Di Chu (Square M/4, Sheet II) does not meet the main watershed at the Diphuk La, but some distance north of it (Vide Sheet 91H). It has been presumed that the boundary should follow the ridge.

"4. The Bhutan-Balipara Frontier Tract boundary has been entered in accordance with the description contained in the printed D.O. letter (No. Pol. 1157/4148-A.P., dated the 29th May, 1936) enclosed with the extracts from your files. *The northern portion has been shown in broken lines to indicate that it is provisional in accordance with Mr. O. K. Caroe's note of the 1st October 1936 included in the extracts now returned. This portion will be marked 'approximate' on published maps".* (The Thagla Ridge is situated just north of this 'approximate' boundary line—*K.G.*).

FURTHER DEBATE ON THE POLICY VIS-A-VIS TAWANG IN 1939

The Governor of Assam, Sir R. N. Reid, wrote a personal letter to the Governor-General Lord Linlithgow on 3rd January, 1939, [I.O.R.: Pol. (External) Dept.: *Collection* 36/File 29. Reid's *Confidential letter* to Linlithgow, dated 3rd January, 1939], making a fresh plea in favour of a second but smaller expedition to Tawang in the following April which would cost only Rs. 25000/-. He said *inter alia*: "..... there are three alternatives. The first is to wash the hands of the whole thing in spite of the fact we told the local people that they were our subjects and not subjects of Tibet. This would save a lot of trouble and expense and, unless there are great changes in the situation in the north, would possibly have no inconvenient consequences for us. But one cannot contemplate with satisfaction a policy of abandoning to their fate people who have been told to regard themselves as dependent upon us. The second alternative is the permanent occupation of Tawang with consequential expenses. Other things being equal, this is a policy which obviously is the most desirable. The third alternative is that to which I have referred above, a further visit on a small scale this spring, but it is no use shutting our eyes to the fact that such a visit, if it is to be worthwhile, would have to be repeated periodically."

Sir Henry Twynum's Letter to the Viceroy

Sir Henry Twynum, who served as the acting Governor of Assam, while Sir R. N. Reid was on home leave in 1939, was not in favour of a 'Forward' policy advocated by the Caroe-Reid school, whose views received support from the explorer Captain Kingdon-Ward (It was his illegal entry into Tibet in 1935 that had roused Olaf Caroe's interest in the Simla Convention 1914— which was till then recognised as an abortive event). Sir Henry Twynum elaborated his views on the Tawang issue in a personal letter to Lord Linlithgow on 17th March 1939 [I.O.R. : Pol. (External) Dept. *Collection* 36/File 23 : *Register No.* 2029/39, *Twynum's letter to Linlithgow,* 17th March, 1939].

TAWANG

"Dear Lord Linlithgow,
 "1. The questions which occur to me are as follows:
 (i) Is the occupation of Tawang necessary or desirable as a matter of high policy as suggested in Kingdon-Ward's article in the journal of the Royal Central Asian Society for October 1938, i.e, in view of possible developments as regards China and Japan ? I understand from the late Lord Brabourne's letter to Hogg dated 23rd July 1938, that the risk of Chinese aggression in this quarter has materially decreased.
 (i) Are we on absolutely firm ground judicially as regards our rights under the Convention of 1914 ?
 "It appears from the Foreign Secretary's letter No. F 433 X/35 dated 18th August 1936 to His Majesty's Under-Secretary of State for India that the *Chinese Government did not ratify the 1914 Convention. If one of the three parties to a Tri-partite Convention does not ratify, can another party to the Convention claim that it is binding between itself and the third party* ?
 "I understand from Your Excellency's letter to Reid, dated 18th May, 1938, that our Treaty rights in the Tawang area are undoubted vis-a-vis Tibet, and I realise that it is advisable to take our stand on the position arrived at in 1914. The following

points are, perhaps, however, relevant as regards affording the Tibetans a loophole, or as presenting difficulties if the matter were referred to arbitration, and I mention them in case the advisability of further negotiation on the subject suggests itself to the External Affairs Department.

"(iii) The map attached to the Convention is on such a small scale that the "red line" is superimposed on the word "Tawang". The actual boundary as now claimed is based upon notes which were exchanged on 24th and 25th March 1914 between Sir Henry McMahon and Lonchen Shatra, the Tibetan Plenipotentiary, which were accompanied by two maps which undoubtedly place Tawang on the British side of the "red line". The Tibetan Plenipotentiary's note dated 25th March 1914 states that he had received orders from Lhasa and accordingly agreed to the boundary. Do we base our claims on these notes, which are lacking in formalities associated with a treaty, or on Article 9 of the Convention which does not refer to the maps accompanying the inter-changed notes, but only to the small scale map attached to the Convention which was subsequently not ratified by China?

"(iv) Does the fact that we took no steps to implement Article 9 of the Convention from 1914 to 1938 affect our position (a) from the point of view of International Law (b) in equity in view of the lapse of time, and altered circumstances?

"(v) It is part of our policy to remain on good terms with Tibet. That being so, is it desirable to press for the inclusion of Tawang salient in British India when perhaps our object could be achieved by fixing the boundary further south possibly at the Digien river? The Dirang Dzong area is sparsely inhabited and its inhabitants are much oppressed by the Akas, while in Kalakthang area, further south, there is a marked change in the characteristics of the inhabitants from Ronnongta, who are true Monbas or low country Bhutias, presumably of Tibetan stock, to Sherchopken who resemble more closely their savage neighbours to the East. Another alternative would be to aim at controlling only the Kalakthang area where the Tsona Jongpens do not collect tribute. It is these two areas which are subject to exactions by the savage Akas. This would involve the limitation of our proposals for ultimate occupation or 'control' to one or two out of three 'distinctive' areas described in Lightfoot's Report, i.e., the Kalakthang area and the sparsely inhabited Dirang Dzong area, but not the Tawang area itself. The limitation of our claims might be used as a diplomatic counter with the Tibetans for formal recognition of boundary just short of the Tawang, and possibly Dirang Dzong, areas and such administrative reforms in those areas as we might consider desirable.

"2. Sir Henry McMahon's note, dated 8th July 1914, shows that the object of including Tawang was to secure (a) a natural watershed frontier (b) access to the shortest trade route into Tibet and control of the monastery of Tawang which had blocked the trade by this route in the past by undue exaction and oppression.

"Further exploration of the country seems to show that objective (a) could be secured by a frontier south of Tawang where the Sela and the Digien River constitute natural boundaries, and objective (b) by negotiation.

"The last paragraph of Sir Henry McMahon's memorandum dated the 28th March 1914 states: "They (the Tibetan Government) have shown a great desire throughout the course of discussions regarding our mutual frontier to show a reasonable and just attitude. Should it be found desirable in the light of the more detailed knowledge which the Tibetan Government and ourselves may acquire in the future to modify the course of the boundary line at any place, we shall doubtless endeavour to show a similar attitude in regard to Tibetan interests, although no obligation to do so has been mentioned in the agreement.

"That was written 25 years ago and has some bearing on the point raised by me in (ii) (b) above in view of the dilatoriness which we have shown in taking steps to investigate the position.

"It seems from the old correspondence that the Tibetan Government were imperfectly acquainted with the position of Tawang and decided the cession without consulting the local landed proprietors or local authorities in the area. This is hardly surprising, when it is considered that the Government was then even more theocratic and medieval than it is now. Last year's exploratory expedition has shown that Tsona Jongpens of Tibet exercise control over Tawang, and to a lesser extent the Dirang Dzong areas. It was known in 1914 that the 'Mon people' paid taxes to Tsona Dzong, but in view of the large measure of local autonomy allowed to Provincial monasteries in Tibet, the implications of this fact were perhaps hardly appreciated by the authorities at Lhasa.

"Humanitarian grounds alone would scarcely be sufficient to justify a 'forward' policy as similar grounds could be urged for the occupation of other areas of Tibet. It is true that last year's expedition may have excited hopes and raised claims, but it is possible that much could be done to fulfil expectations without going so far as to occupy an area which has always been oriented towards Tibet ethnographically, politically and in religion and is even now in Lightfoot's words "dominated by representatives of the Tibetan Government."

"Possible alternatives are (a) the establishment of a Control area to include Dirang Dzong and Kalkthang areas, or possibly the latter area only, (b) posting a native Trade Agent at Tawang to represent our interests there, (c) establishment of a frontier post to safeguard the inhabitants of the Control area from the Akas and Daflas....

"The crux of the whole question—apart from the financial aspect—appears to lie in Lhasa's reactions to a 'forward' policy and the extent to which these should be allowed for...."

TWYNUM'S NOTE RECEIVES RESPONSE FROM VICEROY AND SECRETARY OF STATE

On the 17th April 1939, the Viceroy Lord Linlithgow wrote a letter to Sir Henry Twynum [I.O.R. : Pol. (External) Dept. : *Collection* 36/File 29. *Lord Linlithgow's private and personal letter to Twynum, dated* 17th April 1939] in which he said *inter alia* : ".... although I do not think that there is any reason to suppose that we are on insecure ground with regard to our Treaty rights, I fully agree with you that from the practical point of view there is no advantage and considerable risk in pressing the matter further with the Tibetan Government." But for financial reasons and the deteriorating international situation (The Munich crisis and the danger of war were hovering over Europe), the Viceroy thought that he could not accept even the moderate proposals for establishing a Control area upto the Tawang-Digien River in order to protect the Monbas from the depredation of the Akas, who lived on their borders or allow Captain Lightfoot to undertake a tour in the Dirang Dzong area with a small escort of the Assam Rifles.

The Secretary of State for India in his letter of 13th July 1939, to the Secretary, External Affairs Department, Government of India, [I.O.R. : Pol. (External) Dept. : *Collection,* 36/File 29, *Register No.* P.Z. 2976/39] acquiesced for the time being in the position resulting from Government of India's prohibition of further expedition to Tawang that year and proposed that the whole question of future policy to be adopted in Tawang area should be reconsidered in a year's time in the light of financial and other conditions then prevailing. He also agreed with the Government of India's view that the Political Officer, Sikkim, was to make no further approach to the Tibetan Government in the matter.

The Secretary of State in his letter to the Viceroy dated 25th July 1939 [I.O.R. : Pol. (External) Dept. : *Collection* 36/ File 29. Paragraph for Secretary of State's letter to Viceroy *included* 25th July, 1939] said, "I notice no mention is made of the suggestion put forward unofficially in Twynum's letter . . . that the possibility should be considered of establishing the frontier ultimately in the neighbourhood of Sela and the Digien River, instead of asserting our full rights under the McMahon Agreement to the whole of the Tawang area. . . . I should be interested to have some expression of your views on Twynum's suggestion."

The Viceroy in his private letter to Lord Zetland, the Secretary of State, dated 24th August 1939 [I.O.R. : Pol. (External) Dept. : *Collection* 36/File 29. Extract from private letter from Lord Linlithgow to Lord Zetland, dated 24th August 1939] explained his position about Sir H. Twynum's proposal thus, ". . . 17. The reason why no reference was made to Twynum's proposal, which you mentioned in paragraph 15 of your letter of 25th July, to establish the frontier ultimately in the neighbourhood of the Sela and the Digien River was that he has not yet put it forward officially. My view is that there is much to be said for his proposal both on general and financial grounds, particularly as he thinks that a boundary on the Sela line would only cost about one-fourth of the expenditure estimated to be necessary, if we were to decide eventually to go right upto the McMahon

Line and include Tawang. The present position is that following your Express Letter of 13th July, we have asked Twynum to hold his hand for a year after which the whole matter will be reviewed. Meanwhile from subsequent reports received from Twynum, it seems possible that it is more urgent to push forward further east of the line of the Lower Siang River (the Brahmaputra) where Tibetan influence shows signs of extending into areas which are purely tribal on an easy line of approach to the border of Assam."

OFFICIALS' CONFERENCE ON THE NORTH EASTERN FRONTIER

On 1st August 1940, a conference was held at the Government House, Shillong (Assam), where all the important officers concerned with the North-East frontier participated, e.g., Governor of Assam, Governor's Secretary, Political Officer, Sikkim, Political Officer, Sadiya Frontier Tract, and Political Officer, Balipara Frontier Tract. They agreed on the point that the Government of India should not press their claims to Tawang and suggested that a more suitable line than the McMahon Line would be one further south, either at the Sela range or further south in the neighbourhood of Dirang Dzong. The Political Officer, Sikkim, as well as the Governor of Assam agreed that in trying to vindicate the McMahon Line with least disturbance to Anglo-Tibetan relations, it would be advisable to get ahead in the Siang and Lohit areas before disturbing the *status quo* in the Tawang, Dirang Dzong and Kalaktang areas. [I.O.R. : Pol. (External) Dept. : *Collection* 36/File 23, *Register No.* P.Z. 5515/1940].

IMPACT OF THE WAR IN THE FAR EAST

By the end of 1941, the entry of Japan into the War created a new and dangerous situation in the North-East Frontier of India. In the meantime, during the winter of 1942 a high dignitary of the Tibetan Government paid a visit to Tawang and tried his best to convince the people in the neighbourhood that the area belonged to Tibet. Also he left a "Tibetan garrison of some kind" in the area [I.O.R. : Pol. (External) Dept. : *Collection* 36/File 23; No. Pol. 3797/43. Extract from Governor of

Assam's Letter to the Viceroy, dated 20th March 1943]. There was also an indirect attempt to bring the Bhutan Government to recognise Tibetan jurisdiction over the Tawang area by entering into negotiations about the repatriation of emigrant Tibetan and Bhutanese subjects to their original homelands. The Government of India put pressure on the Tibetan Government through their representative at Lhasa, Mr Ludlow, to withdraw their military forces from Tawang. [I.O.R. : Pol. (External) Dept. : Collection 36/File 23; No. Ext. 1695/1943. Cypher Telegram from G.O.I. External Affairs Department to Secretary of State for India, 1st April 1943].

Anglo-U.S. Difference On Status of Tibet

The British Embassy in Washington D.C. tried to convince the State Department, U.S.A., through their *Aide Memoire* dated 19th April, 1943, [*Foreign Relations of the United States, 1943* : *China* (Department of State, Washington) pp. 626-628] that "The Government of India have always held that the Tibet is a separate country in full enjoyment of local autonomy entitled to exclusive diplomatic representation with other Powers . . . ." The U.S. Department of State, however, held a different view about the status of Tibet which they made clear in their *Aide Memoire* dated 15th May 1943 : ". . . . the Government of the United States has borne in mind that the Chinese Government has long claimed suzerainty over Tibet and that the Chinese Constitution lists Tibet among areas constituting the territory of the Republic of China. This Government has at no time raised a question regarding either of these claims. The Government of the United States does not believe that a useful purpose would be served by opening at this time a detailed discussion of the status of Tibet." [*Ibid.,* p. 630].

Under the circumstances, it became impossible to make good the McMahon Line frontier through diplomatic pressure on the Tibetan Government. The Government of India then decided to postpone their advance to Tawang, as it would irritate the Tibetans to such an extent that they might bring it to the notice of the Chinese, who were then on very friendly terms with the U.S.A.

British Expeditions In Tribal Areas In 1940's

In 1943, J. P. Mills led a mission to establish advanced posts in the unadministered territory of the North-East Frontier. But the advance post he set up in the Tawang sector was at Dirang Dzong. He revealed in his lecture to the Royal Central Asian Society in early 1950 that "our (the British) claim to this country was strenuously opposed by Tibetan secular frontier officials and by monastic collectors. The monastic officials kept a most unpleasant prison at Dirang Dzong, a really humble place, and had not infrequently inflicted the most brutal punishments. They were in fact oppressing the inhabitants to such an extent that a considerable number of them had left their villages and gone away into Bhutan". In the Subansiri area, he found that the tribes were perpetually raiding one another for slaves and the feuds went on endlessly. In the Siang valley, which was densely populated Abor country, J. P. Mills came to learn about the activities of the Tibetan 'tax-collectors' or marauders. The Lohit valley provided a trade route to the Mishmis and Tibetans. In Rima, which was admittedly Tibetan territory, J. P. Mills met a Tibetan official "who claimed as the boundary an imaginary line few miles downstream of the correct one". This was apparently at Menilkrai where the Chinese Army had put up a border sign post in 1910. [J. P. Mills, "Problem of the Assam-Tibet Frontier", *Journal of Royal Central Asian Society* (April, 1950)].

In 1944 Dr Von Haimendorf and his wife led an expedition into the Subansiri region which was till then almost unexplored. This eastern part of the Balipara Frontier Tract was detached and formed into a separate charge under the name of the Subansiri area. In the winter of 1945 Dr Haimandorf led a punitive expedition against a group of Dafla villages who had raided the Apa Tanis, another small peaceable tribe [C. von Furer-Haimendorf, *Himalyan Barbary* (London : John Murray 1955) Introduction, p. xi]. In 1946, Dr and Mrs U. Betts served in this region. In her lecture before the Royal Central Asian Society in early 1949, she gave out that the region till then remained inaccessible, and little could be done in opening up those areas.

Evidence Available in the Officials' Report (1961)

The report of the Chinese officials notes [*Report of the Officials of the Government of India And The People's Republic of China on the Boundary Question*], "After the invasion of the British troops, the Tibet local Government made constant representation with the British, demanding the withdrawal of the invading British forces. For instance, in a meeting with Richardson, the British representative in Lhasa, on May 17, 1944, the Tibet local Goverment pointed out that Britain had dispatched troops to invade such places as Dirang Dzong, obstructed the administration of Tibetan local officials and placed watch on the local inhabitants with its troops to prevent them from rendering services and paying taxes to the Tibetan local government". It also declared : "How could these unprecedented new acts have their origin in the instructions of the Indian Government... It is hoped that the original boundary of the Monyul area would be maintained as before and that the Sinhpa (i.e. British) officers and men may be withdrawn." Thereafter, the Tibetan local government continued to make repeated representations. For instance, in the winter of 1944 and in April 1945, it made two representations, one orally and the other in written form, with the British representative in Tibet, demanding that British troops be withdrawn at once from Kalaktang under the jurisdiction of Taklung Dzong in the southern part of Monyul and from Walong in Lower Tsayul. (p. C.R. 105). ". . . In his conversation with the officials of the Tibet local government on October 11, 1944, Gould, British Political Officer in Sikkim, admitted that with regard to Kalaktang in the Monyul area, the British Indian Goverment 'had not' previously 'exercised special administration over this area', but to from a pretext for Britain's occupation of the Monyul area, he invented the unfounded lie to the effect that 'in view of the fact that recently the Chinese harboured intentions to occupy some places in Burma'. On December 4 of the same year, in his conversation with the local officials of the Tibet region, Gould further stated that 'he was instructed to say that the officials sent by the Indian Government (i.e., the officers and men who occupied Kalaktang and Walong) were not in a position to withdraw. Therefore, it was hoped that the Tibet Government would give up minor considerations for broader interests, be far-sighted and instruct the Tzona Dzong etc. not to collect governmental taxes and corvee in the locality.' In the memorandum which Gould handed on the same day to the local authorities of the Tibet region, it was stated that the British Indian Government insisted on the so-called McMahon Line which was illegally drawn and had never been recognised by the Chinese Government; but it also indicated that 'My Government was willing to change the boundary, namely that starting from Sela, it should run not to the north, but to the south of Tawang,' and demanded that 'the Officials of the Tibet Government be instructed not to exercise authority south of Sela'. This proposal clearly shows that upto the end of 1944, the Tibet local govermnent was still fully exercising its powers of administration in the entire Monyul area; at the same time it shows that the British Indian Government still had some hesitations about invading the northern part of Monyul, north of Sela. But, since it still insisted on occupying the southern part of Monyul, this aggressive proposal was never approved by the Tibetan local government." (p. CR-106).

The Chinese officials' report also said, "Concurrent to its invasion of the Monyul area, Britain dispatched other troops around 1944 to go upto the Tsangpo River and invade the area of Karko and Simong of Loyul." (p. CR-107). "..After receiving the report of the Sera Monastery, the Tibet local government repeatedly ordered the local officials of the Pemakoe to exercise their administrative powers and collect taxes in the Loyul area as they had always done ... In 1946-47, Britain dispatched troops to further occupy the area south of Kapang La and north of Karko and further undermined the administrative power of Tibet" (*Ibid*. p. 108). Concerning the Lower Tsayul area, the Chinese report said, "Starting from 1944, Britain dispatched troops to invade the Walong area of Lower Tsayul ... after Walong was invaded by British troops, the local authorities of the Tibet region negotiated time and again with the British demanding the withdrawal of British troops. On learning of these acts of British aggression, the then Chinese Government sent four notes of protest to the British Embassy in China in July, September and November 1946 and January of 1947 respectively. As Britain shifted the responsibility onto India, the Chinese Government addressed a note of protest to the Indian Embassy in China in February 1947". (*Ibid.,* CR-110).

The chequered history of the North-eastern frontier of India during the days of the British Raj shows that Independent India in 1947 inherited a difficult legacy and her claim to the McMahon Line had no firm basis in international Law.

SARDAR K. M. PANIKKAR AND THE FORMATIVE PHASE OF INDIAN FOREIGN POLICY

It was a strange coincidence of events that the first public feelers about the American plan to move the Seventh Fleet to the Indian Ocean for a 'feel' of its waters came about at a time when India lost one of her foremost foreign policy theorists, who had persistently advocated since 1943 the supreme need for India to develop as a maritime Power so as to be able to ensure the security of the Indian Ocean area, in association with Britain and the Commonwealth.

Sardar Panikkar was the first among the present generation of Indian publicists to point out to their countrymen the vital importance of the Indian Ocean to our security at a time when the leaders of the National Congress still engrossed in the national struggle had no time to examine in full perspective the problem of free India's defence on the basis of geographic realities. Sardar Panikkar wrote in his book *"India And The Indian Ocean"* (1945) : "The peninsular character of the country with its extensive and open coast line, and with a littoral which is extremely fertile and rich in resources, makes India entirely dependent on the Indian Ocean over which her vast trade, has for the most part, found its way to the marts of the world all through history" (p. 82).

While to the other countries, the Indian Ocean is only one of the important oceanic areas, to India it is the vital sea. Her life lines are concentrated in that area. Her future is dependent on the freedom of that vast water surface. No industrial development, no commercial growth, no stable political structure is possible for her unless the Indian Ocean is free and her own shores are fully protected. On the basis of the above argument Sardar Panikkar concluded, "The Indian Ocean must, therefore, remain truly Indian" because the danger to the security of the Indian Ocean may come by the way of the Atlantic as well as the Pacific Ocean, as also by the way of the Persian Gulf.

He said, "A renovated and triumphant China with her population irresistibly moving south from Tonkin to Singapore may become a greater menace to the Indian Ocean than even

Japan with her lines of communication extending so far from the sources of her power". [*Strategic Problems of The Indian Ocean*, p. 9 (1944)]. He reminded his countrymen that the Chinese had a long-naval tradition. In the fifteenth century, Chinese fleets visited Indian ports. The naval power of the Sri Vijayas and later the naval power of the Portuguese in the Indonesian archipelago prevented the southward expansion of China over the Oceanic space. He said in 1945, "That movement towards the south, which is indicated by the significant demography of the area may, in all probability, be reflected in the naval policy of resurgent China". In this context, he also referred to the strategic position of Indo-China: "If, as is possible, Indo-China falls after the war within the Chinese sphere of influence, her authority over the southern waters will clearly be dominant" (*India And The Indian Ocean*, p. 86).

Panikkar also reminded his countrymen in 1945, "... powerful interests in the U.S.A. are urging on the Administration that it is necessary to have more island bases in order to ensure American naval preponderance in the Pacific" (*Ibid.* p. 86). He also assessed, "The naval power of the U.S.A. is already such as to make it a factor in any part of the 'Indivisible Sea'." Panikkar also dealt with other factors which might draw the U.S.A. to the Indian Ocean. "America has developed considerable interests in the Middle East. Oil concessions in Saudi Arabia and in Iran, not to speak of the Bahrein islands—indicate the growth of strong economic interests in the drainage area of the Indian Ocean. America will emerge out of the present war with global and not hemispheric ideas of strategy, and the possibility, therefore, has to be visualised of America entering the Indian Ocean as a major naval Power". (*Ibid.*, p. 87).

Panikkar also deliberated upon the possibility of a Russian entry into the Indian Ocean through the Persian Gulf. He said, "The political, industrial and military organisation of Central Asia under the Soviets gives a new content to the old Russian conception of unrestricted entry into the open sea ... The lines of traffic developed for the purpose of Lend-Lease aid to Russia in the present war demonstrated the vital importance of the Persian Gulf to the Soviets .... The possibility of the presence of a naval Power of the magnitude, resources and persistence of Russia on the Persian Gulf is in itself to revolutionise the strategy in respect of the Indian Ocean". (*Ibid.*, pp. 88-9).

Panikkar could foresee that for a long time to come (for at least another half century) free India's Navy would not be in a position to police the Indian Ocean by herself. He suggested, "The control of the Indian Ocean, must, therefore, be a cooperative effort of India and Britain and other Commonwealth units having interest in the Ocean with the primary responsibility lying on the Indian Navy to guard the steel ring created by Singapore, Ceylon, Mauritius and Socotra." (*Ibid.*, p. 95).

Considering the land defence of India, Panikkar wrote in 1943, "The growth of the military power of the Soviets on the North-West frontier has raised new problems... With the ever-increasing range of bombers, the cities of North-Western India will be open to effective attack." (*The Future of South-East Asia*, p. 30) [This problem arising from the proximity to the Soviet Power was partially resolved by the creation of Pakistan in the north-west region of the Indian sub-continent in 1947].

Panikkar also warned, "The growth of China as a military Power and the recent shifting of the bases of its economic and military organisation to the South-East create equally difficult problems for India." (*The Future of South-East Asia*, p. 30).

Panikkar suggested the creation of a 'Triune Commonwealth' of Hindustan, Pakistan and Burma as one major step for the defence of the Indian sub-continent. Referring to the defence of Burma, he stressed the fact that "it is India's primary concern no less than Burma's to see that its frontiers remain inviolate. In fact no responsibility can be too heavy for India when it comes to the question of defending Burma". (*Ibid.*, p. 41).

The old Indian Empire, according to Panikkar, had much in its favour as a Common Defence Area. It included Aden as an outpost, kept the Persian Gulf and the coast within the orbit of Indian policy, neutralised Tibet and held strongly to the eastern frontier of Burma. He lamented the gradual break-up of the defence scheme beginning with the surrender of Aden to the Colonial Office. He wrote in 1943, "The transfer of the Persian Gulf to the Foreign Office, the separation of Burma and the weakening of the Indian policy towards Tibet and the culmination of British Indian influence in Kashgar were the other steps which have in a period of ten years weakened the defence position of India" (*Ibid.*, p. 45). In the light of the experience of the Second World War which was still on, he concluded that a Curzonian concept of a greater Moghul Empire in Delhi was no longer a possibility. ". . . what is possible is that on the basis of equality and freedom Pakistan, Hindustan and Burma should be united as a single defence area, held together and strengthened by co-operation with Britain to form a great structure for peace and security in Asia." (*Ibid*, p. 46).

Writing again in 1946 in his book *"The Basis of An Indo-British Treaty"*, Panikkar brought in Mackindar's geo-political concepts to confirm his ideas about free India's defence. India, geographically, occupies the peninsular as well as the continental position. But India has no future as a major Asian Land Power, for by land she can be no more than an appendage of only minor interest to the Soviet Union which controlled the Heartland. India must of necessity align herself with the Maritime System. To quote Sardar Panikkar, "The essential fact is that India is a Maritime State with a predominant interest in the sea. She is of the true Rimland, whose continental affiliations are comparatively negligible. From the continental point of view of Eurasia, she is only an abutting corner, walled off by impassable mountains. From the sea and air point of view on the other hand, she is one of the great strategic centres. From the maritime point of view, she dominates the Indian Ocean. From the air point of view, she is claimed to be an 'air island'. She is the natural air transit centre of the maritime areas. To the Maritime State system, India is invaluable. To the continental system she is unimportant". (p. 5).

In 1947, Sardar Panikkar published two papers in the *India Quarterly* (Vol. 1 and 2) on "The Himalayas and Indian Defence". He pointed out therein that in the days of air power, the effectiveness of the Himalayas as a protective barrier to India no longer held good as in the past. He said, "If the pure geographical definition of the Himalayas as having the width of only 150 miles is taken, that is to say, if it were possible to isolate the range and forget the (Tibetan) plateau to the north, the Himalayas—in spite of their immense height—should not be an effective barrier." But, he added, "the essential point about the Himalayas is not their width of 150 miles, but the plateau behind it, which in itself is an elevation of about 15000 feet and is guarded on all four sides by high mountains. In fact, the vast barrier upland behind the Himalayas provides the most magnificent defence in depth imaginable. No centre of dynamic power can be created anywhere near the ranges. The climatic conditions above the plateau are most unsuited and unfavourable for air operations and the distance involved from any reasonable point where enemy can concentrate and deliver a continuous attack on the Himalayan side is so great as to be negligible."

As regards the land defence, he concluded, "The creation of a broader no-man's land on both flanks of the Himalayas will give to the Indian peninsula sufficient area for the development of her defence potential free from interference".

He also touched the point of naval defence in these papers. He said, "If the control of the sea is lost, not only could she be blockaded and her economic life subjected to slow strangulation, but the centres of her industry pounded out of existence by carrier-borne aircraft.... The control of the Indian Ocean alone will save India from disaster from blockade, seaborne invasion and destruction of economic life from air attack."

The partition of India in August 1947 with two flanks of Pakistan serving as a new type of 'Cordon Sanitaire', weakened the defence potential of India to a large extent. The Communist Revolution in China in October 1949, which almost coincided with the first atomic explosion in Russia, together with the Sino-Soviet Treaty (February 1950) brought about a geopolitical shift in the world balance of power. As a result, many of the presumptions on which Sardar Panikkar built up his theory of Indian defence and foreign policy became outdated very soon after the transfer of power in India. Even then, we find an impress of his idea on Indian foreign policy, especially in the formative stage.

One of the first steps by free India to ensure the security of the Indian Ocean was to recall the Indian armed forces from South-East Asian countries where they had been despatched by the British authorities to suppress the national liberation movements in the interests of the European Colonial Powers. Also Nehru took the lead in organising the first Asian Relations Conference in New Delhi in March-April 1947, the object of which was to rouse a collective voice of protest against the recrudescence of Western Imperialism in Asia—especially in the countries of the region of the Indian Ocean.

On the other hand, when Communism appeared to be an ascendent force in Malaya, Burma and Indo-China in 1948, the Government of India refused to be enamoured of the anti-colonial nature of these Communist movements. The strategic position of Malaya in the defence of the Indian Ocean as elaborated by Panikkar might have been taken into consideration when the Government of India soft-pedalled British imperialism in Malaya, nay more than that, provided transit facilities to Gurkha soldiers for the suppression of the Communist (Chinese) rebellion in Malaya.

The Government of India rushed to the aid of the Burma Government in 1949, when as a result of the Communist-Karen revolt, the Government under U Nu lost control over the major portion of its territory, and its authority remained limited to a few major towns alone. The Government of India called a Commonwealth Conference in Delhi to arrange for financial aid to the Government of Burma in distress and sent supplies of small arms to the U Nu Government.

The Government of India did not extend recognition to the Communist-oriented Government of Indo-China under Dr Ho Chi-Minh, although it recognised him as the head of the anti-colonial struggle against the French imperialism in Indo-China and regarded the Bao Dai Government as a French protege.

On the other hand, in the case of Dutch aggression on Indonesia (1947-49), the Government of India took various positive steps, including the calling of the Asian Conference on Indonesia in January 1949, in which two Commonwealth Powers, Australia and New Zealand, were associated. The emergence of a friendly non-communist Indonesia was highly important in India's defence strategy in the Indian Ocean.

On the seaboard of the Indian Ocean in West Asia, as well as East Africa, the Government of India took a rather lenient view of the British presence in Iran, Iraq, Oman, Aden, Suez, Kenya, and also in Cyprus. Even after the Suez invasion in the fall of 1956, the Government of India tried its best (after the collapse of the Franco-British misventure) to heal the breach between Egypt and Britain so as to restore normal relationship.

The Government of India has been generally more critical about the French and Portuguese imperialism in East and North Africa. Also the Government of India was strongly opposed to the American entry into West Asia through the proposed MEDO, Eisenhower Doctrine, the Baghdad Pact or the CENTO, (as also entry into South-East Asia through the SEATO). In 1946, the Congress Party expressed its disapproval of the Russian presence in the North Iran, although in a garbed language. Nehru did not approve the U.S. intervention in Indo-China in June 1950 in the wake of the Korean war and strongly opposed the proposed U.S. military intervention in the critical phase of the war in Indo-China in 1954.

The most important foreign policy decision about the continuance of the Commonwealth membership was taken by the Government of India in April 1949. Considering the strength of the anti-Commonwealth sentiment prevalent in India, forcefully subscribed to by Nehru himself (Cf. *The Discovery of India,* 1945), the Government of India's decision to maintain close ties with Britain through the Commonwealth was at least partially influenced by the ideas of defence strategy propagated by Sardar Panikkar during 1943-47. According to Professor Gurmukh Nihal Singh, speaking at the Indian Council of World Affairs on 3rd May, 1949, "the problem of defence and the onrush of Communism in Asia must have been among the reasons that influenced the Government of India to remain in the Commonwealth".

It would be, however, wrong to overstress the influence of any particular publicist on the formulation of free India's foreign policy, which was so largely Prime Minister Nehru's own making. But it is interesting to study the ideas of Sardar Panikkar in the formative phase of our foreign policy, since it helps us to find some clues to certain anamolies and apparent contradictions in the working of Indian foreign policy which was officially declared to be based on certain abstract principles such as : (1) Nonalignment with Power Blocs, (2) Support to the principle of freedom for Colonial peoples, and (3) Opposition to racial discrimination.

As a diplomat representing India in two Chinas, Sardar Panikkar attained both celebrity as well as notoriety. A proper assessment of his contribution to Indian diplomacy can be made only when the Government of India opens the secret files of the External Affairs Ministry relating to his period of Ambassadorship in China during 1948-52, the momentous period of the Korean War which tended to escalate into a World War on several occasions. This was also the period of establishment of Chinese sovereignty over Tibet after 40 years of effective sterilisation, which posed before free India the tremendous problem of a 'Live Border' of about 2000 miles along the Himalayas. It is time that the career of such a colourful but controversial personality as Panikkar's should be studied at a scholarly level particularly as rethinking about the basic premises of our foreign policy has began. The Government of India can help by making the files relating to our China policy, during the period of Panikkar's Ambassadorship, open for study.

PART II

1. THE KOREAN CRISIS AND THE UNITED NATIONS
2. A NEW LOOK INTO THE ORIGIN OF THE KOREAN WAR
3. ORIGIN OF THE KOREAN WAR AND INDIA'S STAND

PART II

1. The Korean Crisis and the United Nations
2. A new look into the origin of the Korean War
3. Origin of the Korean War and India's stand

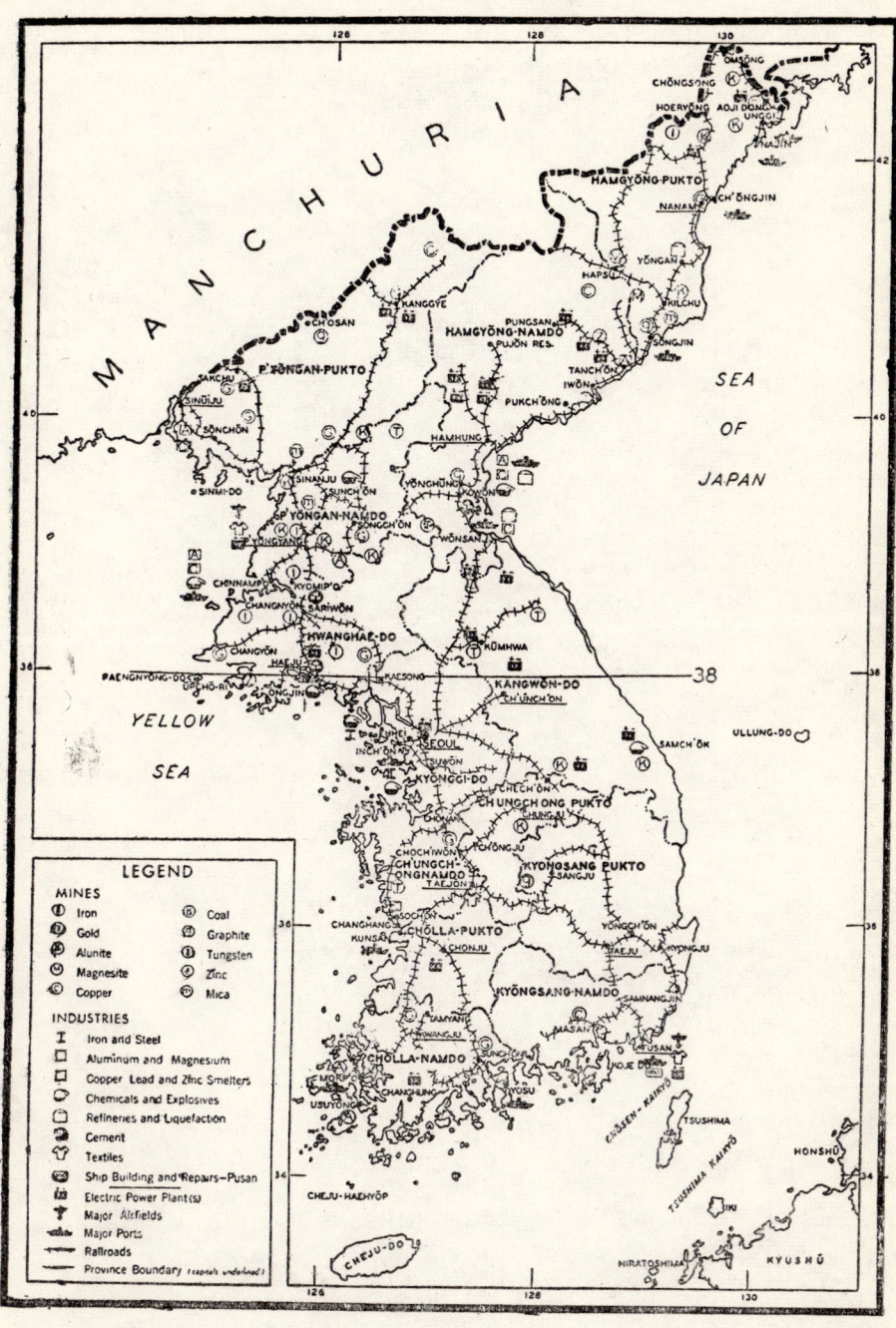

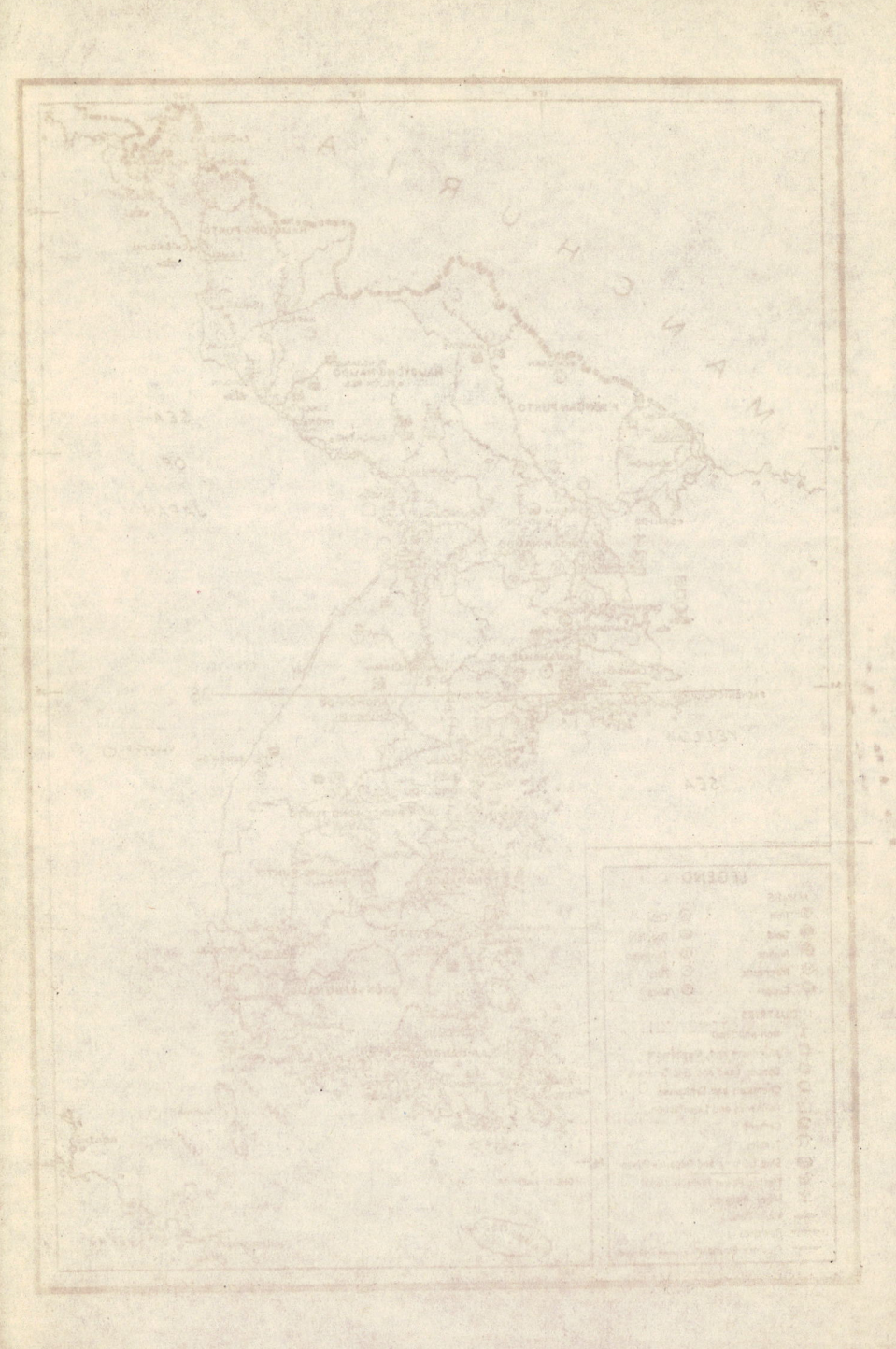

THE KOREAN CRISIS AND THE UNITED NATIONS

A breach of peace occurred in Korea on 25th June, 1950, when large-scale fighting started across the 38th Parallel between the Republic of Korea in the South and the People's Democratic Republic of Korea in the North which were the protégés of the U.S.A. and the U.S.S.R. respectively. On the same date, the U.S. representative in the Security Council brought the Korean situation to the notice of the UN Secretary-General, who arranged for an immediate meeting of the Security Council.

We may note, however, that the problem of the independence of Korea has been in the agenda of the UN General Assembly since 17 September 1947, following a rift between the U.S.A. and the U.S.S.R. about the procedure of establishing a free and independent Korea as envisaged in the Cairo and Potsdam declarations. In August 1945, on the eve of the collapse of the Japanese Army when the victorious Soviet Army was over-running the Korean peninsula, the Soviet Union agreed to an American proposal that the Soviet Army should accept military surrender from the Japanese forces north of the 38th Parallel, while the American Army would accept south. This division of Korea in 1945 into two occupation Zones across the 38th Parallel continued since then.

Introduction of the Korean issue, a matter relating to Peace Treaties, in the General Assembly in September 1947, was opposed by the Soviet Union under Art. 107 of the UN Charter. The U.S. spokesman quoted Art. 11, Para 2, and Art. 14 to score his point. Later the Soviet delegate demanded that the elected representative of the Korean people be summoned before the UN Assembly. Then the defeated Soviet Bloc pursued a policy of non-co-operation alleging that decisions were being taken in the General Assembly, without inviting the Korean representatives to take part in the deliberations. On 14 November 1947, the Assembly set up a Temporary Commission to supervise free elections *throughout Korea* so that an independent *National Government of Korea* might be formed.

As a result of Soviet opposition, UNTCOK was debarred from entering into North Korea. On the advice of the Interim

Committee (a body declared illegal by the Soviet Bloc), the UNTCOK observed an election held in South Korea in May, 1948. (Most members of the UNTCOK originally had had genuine doubts whether it was legally open to them to implement the resolution of the General Assembly (November 1947) in one part of Korea only). The Republic of Korea was established in August, 1948, under the Presidency of Syngman Rhee. In September, the People's Democratic Republic of Korea was set up in the Soviet model in North Korea under Kim Il Sung. The Soviet Army left North Korea in December 1948, leaving an well-organised Army and supplies. The American Army left South Korea in June 1949, leaving 500 Military advisers and providing for adequate funds to meet the current deficits in the Government budget.

Tension between these two Korean client-states continued unabated and there was much military posturing across the Parallel from both sides. The UN Commission on Korea, which had taken the place of the Temporary Commission, called for UN Military Observers in early June 1950, to report on the situation at the 38th Parallel. This was the background of the conflict in Korea.

The UN Secretary-General Trygve Lie, on receipt of an information about an armed invasion of South Korea on 25th June 1950, by the North Korean forces from the US delegate, called for an immediate report from the UNTCOK about the situation.

The UNTCOK in its first cablegram passed on the statement of Syngman Rhee that attacks had been launched in strength all along the Parallel, and also referred to the Pyongyang Radio announcement at 1-35 p.m. about South Korean invasion across the Parallel during the night—which was declared entirely false by Syngman Rhee and his Foreign Minister. ("Material essential to the refutation of the Communist charge that the North Koreans were defending themselves against aggression is still not available"—*Defence in the Cold War*, by A Chatham House Study Group, p. 110).

I. U.N. ACTION IN KOREA

At the Security Council meeting on 25th June, 1950, Chairman of the Council, Sir B. N. Rau, invited the representative of the Government of the Republic of Korea to sit at the Council table and submit a statement at the request of the US delegate. The Security Council, however, did not extend that opportunity to the Government of North Korea.

The Security Council passed an American sponsored resolution as modified by a UK amendment on 25th June 1950, in which the Council noted "with grave concern the armed attack on the Republic of Korea by the forces from North Korea" and declared that "this action constitutes a breach of peace" and called for an immediate cessation of hostilities and withdrawal of North Korean forces to the 38th Parallel. The UNTCOK was asked to communicate its fully considered recommendation on the situation.

On the 26th June, the UNTCOK gave its verdict that North Korea was carrying out a full-scale invasion on the basis of the Military Observers' Report (The two Australian Military Observers had left the 38th Parallel on 23rd June, two days before the hostilities were first reported. But their report was submitted on 26th June, one day after the armed conflict started. Their report does not provide any direct evidence about the origin of war at the 38th Parallel on 25th June, and only puts stress on the absence of military concentration in forward areas in South Korea indicating their incapability to launch offensive operations. This report has been subsequently contradicted by General MacArthur in his evidence before the joint Committee of the US Senate in May, 1951) and recommended invitation to both parties to agree on a neutral mediator either to negotiate peace, or requesting member Governments to undertake immediate mediation.

On 29th June, President Truman ordered US naval and air force to give assistance to the Republic of Korea (and neutralise Formosa against Communist invasion), before the Security Council met and recommended that "the members of the United Nations furnish such assistance to the Republic of Korea as may be necessary to repel the armed attack and restore international peace and security in the area." Apparently these Security Council resolutions were in consonance with the Charter (Art. 39 & 40). [It was necessary for the Security Council action, however, that the then 'absence' of the U.S.S.R. under protest on the question of Chinese representation, should be interpreted as equivalent to 'abstention' by a Great Power. This interpretation is controversial (cf. Prof. Leo Gross in *Yale Law Journal*, February 1951).]

After initial military reverses, the UN forces, placed under the Unified Command of the United States by the Security Council resolution of 7th July, finally succeeded in reversing the tide of North Korean advance and threw the North Korean forces across the 38th Parallel by the end of September, 1950.

In October 1950, the UN forces marched into North Korea to establish "peace and security in the area" under a General Assembly resolution dated 7th October 1950. This brought forth massive intervention by the Chinese 'Volunteers', which drove the UN forces back well below the Parallel. In November 1950, the General Assembly passed the US sponsored "Uniting For Peace" resolution providing for emergency sessions of the Assembly in case of aggression—real or threatened, when the Security Council was unable to function due to lack of unanimity among the Big Five. The General Assembly also passed a resolution on 1st February 1951, branding Communist China as an aggressor.

These measures had no apparent effect on the military situation. Since April 1951, there was a stalemate in battle and armistice negotiations were started in Punmunjon in July 1951. In July 1953, an armistice agreement was signed on the basis of the cease-fire line which roughly corresponded with the 38th Parallel, providing for a Political Conference to settle allied problems. It may be noted that the Korean war passed through several phases from 25th June 1950 to 28th July 1953. It began as a fight between North Korea and South Korea. Then came the US intervention closely followed by UN support. When the UN forces were planning to march up to the Yalu, the Foreign Minister of Communist China declared that the crossing of the 38th Parallel by the US forces would result in an extension of the area of conflict. This warning was conveyed to the UN through the Indian Government but was ignored. The UN forces marched up. In November 1950, the entry of the Chinese 'Volunteers' started a new phase. Henceforth, the main antagonists were not the North Koreans and the South Koreans but the Americans and the Chinese whether on the battle field or in the armistice negotiations.

II. Appraisal of the Effectiveness of UN Action in Korea

The UN action in Korea has been judged very differently by various students of public affairs. Trygve Lie, Dulles, Dean Acheson, Adlai Stevenson considered that the operation in Korea was a more or less successful effort in collective security. On the other hand, Senator Taft held the opposite view. If we, however, agree with President Truman's view that "The attack on Korea makes it plain beyond all doubt that Communism has passed beyond the use of subversion to conquer independent nations, and will now use armed invasion and war", (27.6.1950), we may perhaps also agree with his statement (7th May 1951) that "the progress of Communist imperialism throughout Asia has been checked by the firm stand of the UN in Korea and that the battle against aggression has dealt a heavy blow to the Kremlin conspiracy outside Asia."

Nehru differed from this view, though he too believed at that time that the Korean war was a clear case of North Korean aggression. [Nehru is reported to have stated in his interview published in *Neuzurche Zeitung* on 27th January, 1956, "A thorough study of documents has rather convinced him to-day that the real motives of this conflict have been in the policy of Dr. Syngman Rhee". (*The Hindustan Times*, 28th January, 1956).]. He had stressed all along that the Korean war must be localised, and brought to a close as soon as the violation of the 38th Parallel was checked.

When the UN forces began their march towards the Yalu, with the sanction of the General Assembly resolution in October 1950, Nehru became cynical about the nature of this United Nations war. He said on 6th December, 1950, "Everybody talks of freedom, the unity and independence of Korea. The forces that are fighting the UN say more or less the same thing but the result of this unanimity of approach, if I may say so, is this : Korea is a dying and desolate contry. It is extraordinary that we should seek to help our friends in ways which kill or destroy them."

It might be said to the credit of the UN action on 27th June, 1950, that it was endorsed by 52 out of 59 member-states. On the other hand, it may be said that the Korean war was a UN war in name only, nineteenth of the non-ROK troops being supplied by the U.S.A. The U.S.A. permitted no effective participation by other UN members in military planning, political decisions or the long-drawn armistice negotiations.

III. OTHER HOSTILITIES AND THE PREVAILING CAUSES OF CONFLICT

Nehru said in Parliament on 29th September 1954, "I am convinced that there would have been no Korean war if the People's Goverment of China had been in the United Nations, because people could have dealt with China across the table." This statement makes it clear that the Korean war was intimately associated with the current Great Power tension in the Far East. This tension was largely the result of the U.S. policy of non-recognition of the People's Republic of China which was the only effective government in the Chinese mainland since the fall of 1949, as also the exclusion of the Communist Government of China from its legitimate position in the UN Security Council as a Permanent member—mainly due to U.S. opposition. Still another cause of tension was the continuation of U.S. aid to bolster up the Kuomintang Government settled in Formosa. This was regarded by the People's Republic of China as continued intervention in the civil war in China by the U.S.A. In fact, the Chinese Communist Government regarded the outbreak of war in Korea in June 1950, as being deliberately precipitated by the U.S. Government to provide a plea for its alleged secret design to establish a permanent protectorate over Formosa.

Truman's decision in coupling military action in Korea with the extension of military protection to Formosa on 27th June, 1950, did not help to eradicate this impression from the mind of the neutral observers.

IV. THE REASONS FOR UN EFFECTIVENSS OR INEFFECTIVENESS IN THE AREA

The original UN action in Korea on 27th June, 1950, designed to stop the North Korean invasion, could be effective due to certain fortuitous circumstances such as the presence of a UN Commission already operating in Korea equipped with military observers, the availability of American troops nearby in Japan, above all the absence of the Soviet delegate (who boy-

THE KOREAN CRISIS AND THE UNITED NATIONS 113

cotted the Security Council Meetings since 13th January 1950 till 31st July 1950, on the issue of Chinese representation), providing an opportunity to by-pass the Soviet veto.

The UN action in Korea became ineffective as soon as it tried to go beyond its original and limited objective to nullify the invasion across the 38th Parallel, and ventured to bring about a forcible unification of Korea ignoring the vital interests of its two great neighbours, the Communist China and the U.S.S.R.

8

A NEW LOOK INTO THE ORIGIN OF THE KOREAN WAR

A. J. P. Taylor once lamented: "In the Cold War apparently even the world of scholarship knows no detachment" (*Manchester Guardian*, 19 January 1961). This statement particularly applies to Korea which became a focus of the East-West Cold War since 1945 and turned into a bitter battle-ground between the supposedly monolithic world Communism and the Western Alliance during 1950-1953.

How did the Korean War begin? The question was crucial in 1950, when on 27th June, within 48 hours of the start of the fighting across the 38th Parallel between the North Koreans and the South Koreans, President Truman answered it with the statement that "Communism has now passed beyond the use of subversion to conquer independent nations, and will now use armed invasion and war." Since then, it has become a shibboleth of political identification; if one replies that North Korea attacked the South, this implies a whole corpus of political attitudes and the opposite reply connotes a contrary political position. But now that more than two decades have passed, it is surely time that an attempt was made to see what answer the evidence offers to the question—how did that war begin?

The Western world had been firmly convinced about the charge of the North Korean aggression because of the circumstantial evidence about the rapid advance of the Northern Army towards Seoul. Few cared to note that on the very day of the start of the War, the two most strategically important towns in Korea adjacent to the 38th Parallel, viz., Kaesong in the South and Haeju in the North respectively, were captured by the hostile forces. While the U.N. Commission on Korea heard the North Korean broadcast on 25 June 1950 alleging the South Korean attack on Haeju, it simply brushed aside that complaint without any enquiry and accepted the South Korean complaint about an unprovoked aggression to be true. In 1967, a Korean scholar Soon Sung Cho wrote in his book *Korea In World Politics* (1940-1950): "Who was mainly responsible for the outbreak of the Korean War? Was it the Soviet Union, the

United States, North or South Korean leaders ? This question is difficult to answer mainly because of the lack of reliable documentary evidence. The answer so far found is more or less based on circumstantial evidence" (p. 270). Uptill now, no scholar has tried to look into the direct evidence to clinch the issue of aggression in the Korean War. A close study of the military situation along the 38th Parallel on 25 June 1950 on the basis of Official *communiqués,* radio broadcasts, and press agency and newspaper reports and U.N. documents should convince any detached scholar that the *prima facie* case for the South's invasion of the North was at *least* as strong as that for the North's invasion of the South. But that because of the pro-U.S. bias of the two U.N. Military Observers (Australian) as also of the U.N. Commission on Korea, and the rail-roading procedures of the Security Council (then dominated by the U.S.A. due to the U.S.S.R. boycotting its meetings on the issue of Chinese representation), the rival claims were never properly considered. In addition, India's proper neutral role was most unfortunately not played on the issue of the origin of the Korean War. (The Indian Chairman of the Council Sir B. N. Rau denied a hearing to the North Korean Government but allowed a South Korean spokesman to present his complaint). India could and should have taken the Yugoslav view that the Council was not in a position to pass immediate judgement on either of the parties involved in view of contradictory information conveyed by the news dispatches, and that before reaching any conclusion the Council ought to have heard a representative of the North Korean Government.

Apart from this lapse of the Security Council, its denying the Government of mainland China access to the United Nations meant that the decisions of the Council on 25 and 27 June, 1950, for collective action against North Korea were taken in the absence of the two Great Powers—China and the USSR—vitally interested in the fate of Korea, as its immediate neighbours. So the motives of the U.S.A. in carrying on war against North Korea under the flag of the United Nations were suspect from the beginning in the eyes of the Communist giants, specially so because of the turning of Formosa into virtually an American protectorate under President Truman's order of 27 June 1950. So the Communist world looked upon the Korean War as a case of

American-inspired aggression, while the Western world looked upon this war as a case of Communist aggression. And there has not yet been any serious attempt by either side to establish its version of the origin of the Korean War on the basis of direct or factual fool-proof evidence.

The Background

Korea—historically a tributary state of the Chinese empire—became a Japanese protectorate in 1895 and then a Japanese colony since 1910. Towards the end of the World War II in the Far East, the Soviet Union joined the war on the side of her allies. In August 1945 on the eve of the collapse of the Japanese Army, when the victorious Soviet Army was over-running the Korean penninsula, the Soviet Union agreed to an *impromptu* American proposal that Korea should be divided into two zones across the 38th Parallel for the purpose of acceptance of military surrender. The parallel was meant to be a purely military mechanism to ensure that, the Japanese north of the line would surrender to the Soviet Union, those south of the line to the United States. "The 38th Parallel makes no political, topographical, geographic, economic, or military sense. It cut right through whole towns, and even, in one case, separated one wing of a factory from another". (John Gunther: *The Riddle of MacArthur*, p. 163). In the context of developing Cold War, however, the 38th Parallel turned into a rigid frontier between two Korean client-states under the influence of the USA and the Soviet Union.

Following a deadlock in Soviet-American negotiations, the Korean issue was introduced in the UN General Assembly in September 1947 on the initiative of the USA in the teeth of Soviet opposition. On 14 November 1947, the Assembly set up a Temporary Commission to supervise free elections "throughout Korea" so that an independent "National Government of Korea" might be set up. As a result of Soviet opposition, UNTCOK was debarred from entering into North Korea. On the advice of the Interim Committee of the General Assembly, a body declared illegal by the Soviet bloc, the UNTCOK, observed an election held in South Korea in May 1948. The Republic of Korea was established in August 1948 south of the 38th Parallel under the presidency of Syngman Rhee. In September 1948, the People's Democratic Republic of Korea was set up in the Soviet model in North Korea under Kim Il Sung. All Soviet troops were withdrawn from North Korea in December 1948. The US army returned from South Korea in June 1949, leaving behind 500 Military Advisers.

Tension between two Koreas continued unabated and there was military posturing across the 38th Parallel from both sides (According to the Hong Kong correspondent of *The New York Times*, Walter Sullivan "The warlike talk strangely has almost come from the South Korean leaders."—*N. Y. Times*, 26 June 1950). Fresh general elections were duly held in South Korea in May 1950 on American insistence, in spite of President Syngman Rhee's reluctance. "Dr. Rhee's party retained only 22 of 210 seats. and control of the Assembly passed to a confused mismash of middle and independent groups" (John Gunther: *The Riddle of MacArthur*, p. 172). On 7th June 1950, the leaders of North Korea appealed to the people of Korea—North and South—for peaceful unification of the country on the basis of general elections to be held throughout Korea on 5-8 August and called for convening a consultative conference for this purpose at Haeju (a North Korean border town) or at Kaesong (a South Korean border town) on June 15-17. But they debarred Syngman Rhee and his close associates from the proposed convention and also precluded any intervention by the UN Commission on Koreas. These initiatives from North Korea, however, created tensions within South Korea and the border region was regarded as more sensitive, so much so that the UN Commission on Korea called for the deployment of UN Military Observers to report on the situation along the 38th Parallel. The arrest of three delegates from the North, who crossed the border to deliver the appeal for peaceful unification of the country to the leaders of the political parties in South Korea on 11 June, added to the prevailing tension. John Foster Dulles, the Special Consultant to the U.S. State Department, arrived in Seoul on 17th June and inspected the South Korean forces deployed near the 38th Parallel. He also addressed the National Assembly on 19th June in which he pledged American support to the Republic of Korea in facing the challenge of Communism. This was another factor in raising the tension to a high pitch across the 38th Parallel.

The Outbreak of the War And The U.N. Commission

The UN Commission on Korea, functioning in the Republic of Korea (South), had its first task to "observe and report any developments which might lead to or otherwise involve military conflict in Korea" as per the General Assembly resolution of 21 October 1949. But the first report about the outbreak of the Korean War which the UN Secretariat received was that sent by the U.S. Ambassador in the Republic of Korea (South) Mr Muccio to the US Secretary of State. The UNCOK seemed to remain unconcerned about the outbreak of the war across the 38th Parallel on 25th June early morning. At 2 P.M. Korean time, the Secretary-General Trygve Lie telegraphed to the UN Commission in Seoul asking for a report. Some hours later the Commission sent a telegram in reply (*UN Document* S/1496), which threw no light on the origin of the fighting, but merely stated that each side accused the other. The Commission suggested to the Secretary-General that he might consider the possibility of bringing the matter to the notice of the Security Council and that the Commission would communicate more fully considered recommendations later.

At the urgent request of the US Government, the Security Council met at Lake Success at 2 P.M. (E.D.T.) on 25 June, (there is a time-lag of 14 hours between Eastern Day light and Korean time, and 9 hours time-lag between Korean time and London time) and after hearing a South Korean delegate adopted a U.S. sponsored resolution declaring that the armed attack by the North Korean forces constituted a breach of peace, and calling for the immediate cessation of hostilities and the withdrawal of the North Korean forces to the 38th Parallel. Also the UN Commission was asked to communicate its fully considered recommendation on the situation with the least possible delay. The Council rejected a draft resolution proposed by Yugoslavia which called for an immediate cessation of hostilities and the withdrawal of forces in Korea and provided for an invitation to be sent to the Government of North Korea to state its case before the Security Council. The Yugoslav delegate vainly pleaded that, since the documents and reports on aggression were not adequate to place a definite responsibility of guilt on either side, the Security Council should, for the time being, ask for the mere cessation of hostilities.

On 26th June, on the basis of the UN Military Observers' Report that the South Korean Army was organised entirely for defence and that they were taken completely by surprise, as also on the basis of the actual progress of operations, the UNCOK gave its verdict that North Korea was carrying out a full-scale invasion. It recommended that the Security Council might invite both parties to agree on a Neutral Mediator either to negotiate peace, or request member Governments to undertake immediate mediation.

On 27th June, President Truman ordered the U.S. Naval and Air forces to support the Republic of Korea (South) against the North Korean invasion and sent the Seventh Fleet to cordon off Formosa as a pre-emptive measure against possible invasion from the Chinese mainland under the control of the People's Republic of China. A few hours later, the Security Council met and adopted a U.S. sponsored resolution, which recommended that "the members of the United Nations furnish such assistance to the Republic of Korea as may be necessary to repel the armed attack and restore international peace and security in the area".

The North Korean Invasion And the Capture of Haeju by South Koreans

With this background of the Korean crisis and the circumstances of the United Nations' intervention in the Korean War in June 1950, it will be easier for us to sift the available evidence on the question of guilt for aggression. From a study of the reports published on *26th June 1950* in the leading British dailies such as *The Times, The Manchester Guardian* and *The Daily Telegraph*, it would appear that the North Korean Army did invade South Korea on 25th June at some unspecified time and captured the border towns *Ongjin* and *Kaesung* as also all the territory in South Korea, West or North-West of the Imjin river. Again from a study of the following (Seoul-dated) reports published on 26th June in the British and American dailies, we find confirmation about the North Korean allegation about a South Korean attack on North Korea on 25th June :

(1) *The Manchester Guardian* :
"The American officials confirmed that the South Korean troops had captured *Haeju*, five miles inside North Korea, near the west coast".

(2) *The Daily Herald* :
American military observers said the South Korean forces made a successful relieving *counter-attack* near the west coast, penetrated five miles into the Northern territory and seized the town of *Haeju*.

"At night fall Lt. Col. Mahoney, Chief of staff of the United States Military Advisory Group, summed up the situation—All southern territory west of the Imjin river lost to a depth of at least three miles inside the border except in the area of *Haeju* counter-attack."

(3) *The News Chronicle* :
"The South Korean Government claims to have *counter-attacked* at one point on the border and to have captured *Haeju*, manufacturing town five miles inside North Korea".

(4) *The Daily Express* (Seoul, Monday morning 26 June) :
"Last night the American-trained forces of the South *counter-attacked* and seized a town five miles inside North Korea."

(5) *The New York Herald Tribune* (26 June, Seoul United Press) :
"Two companies of picked South Korean troops drove across the 38th Parallel, which forms the frontier, to capture the manufacturing town of *Haeju* just north of the line. The Republican troops captured quantities of equipment, including 10 trucks and about a 100 light machine guns."

(6) *The New York Times* (26 June, Seoul) :
"This morning, according to South Korean office of Public Information, South Korean troops pushing northward captured *Kaeju* (?) capital of Wranghae (?) Province, which is one mile north of the border, taking 10 anti-aircraft piece and ten trucks."

(7) *The Chicago Tribune* (26 June, Seoul Associated Press) :
This carried a report on the front page to the effect that a town had been taken five miles north of the Parallel (See Glenn D. Paige : *The Korean Decision* (June 24-30, 1950) p. 130 fn.).

According to the UNCOK Report submitted to the Secretary-General on 26th June 1950, a radio broadcast from Pyongyang at 1-35 P.M. on 25th June 1950, claimed that South Korea having rejected every Northern proposal for peaceful unification crowned its iniquity by launching an invasion force across the parallel in the section of Haeju, thus precipitating North Korean counter-attack. The UNCOK, however, did not care to verify this allegation by the North Koreans about the attack on *Haeju* by the Southern forces and just brushed it aside and said *"The Commission has no evidence to justify in any respect of the Northern allegations"*. (*UN Document S/ 1505/ Rev. 1*).

The seriousness of this omission on the part of the UNCOK would be crystal clear only if we have an idea of the importance of *Haeju* in the geography of divided Korea, also its significance as a centre of population. Unfortunately in 1950, there were few scholars in the West who had knowledge of Korean geography—Korea being a Japanese colony for about half-a-century. According to *The Columbia-Lippincott Gazetteer Of The World* (1952), (p. 972), *Haeju* is one of the seven major centres of population in North Korea. A close look at the map of Korea would show that *Haeju* is the only major centre in North Korea adjacent to the 38th Parallel, other major centres, viz., Pyongyang, Wonsan, Hamhung, Chongjin, Sinuiju and Chinnampo being far above the Parallel. According to this *Gazetteer*, the population of *Haeju* was above 82000 on the basis of the 1944 census (*Ibid*, p. 743). *Haeju* was the capital of Korea until 1392 A.D. and is now the capital of Hwanghae Province. The town of *Haeju* is rectangular in shape and is surrounded by a defensive wall. (Vide Lautensach's German publication : *Korea*, 1945, p. 272). *Haeju* is a commercial centre for gold-mining and an agricultural area. It is an important centre of ginsen (a herb widely used in Chinese medicine) production. *Haeju* is also a manufacturing town with cement, gold-refining, heavy chemicals, iron industry and electric power plants. *Haeju* is also a major port.

A more significant point about *Haeju*, the town captured by the South Koreans on the very day of the start of the war, is the fact that *Haeju* is the only railway junction just above the Parallel, leading directly to Pyongyang, the capital of North Korea—65 miles away—by the shortest route available. *Haeju* is also linked to Pyongyang by a road. (The map prepared by the U.S. Information Service in the U.K. in 1950 shows only the motor road between Haeju and Pyongyang, omitting the railway link, though the U.S. Army Map of Korea as well as other standard atlases show *Haeju* as a railway junction linked to Pyongyang). The map of Korea shows that two railway lines from the South Korean border towns Ongjin and Kaesung cut across the 38th Parallel to converge on *Haeju,* which would be a gateway to any projected assault on Pyongyang from South Korea. From the view point of the North Koreans, the town of *Haeju*—which provides a railway as well as a road link from South Korea to their capital Pyongyang only 65 miles away—must have been the key centre in their defence strategy for the security of their capital city. So an assault on *Haeju* on 25th June 1950, might reasonably be regarded by North Koreans as an attempt by Syngman Rhee to fulfil his oft-repeated boast about capturing Pyongyang within three days, especially in the context of the recent visit of J. F. Dulles to South Korea and firm assurance of American support given by him. Dulles said in the South Korean Assembly on 19th June, "South Korea would never be alone so long as it continued to play a worthy part in the fight for human freedom. The Republic which confronted the menace of Soviet Communism across its boundary had proved that the task was not hopeless." (*The Times,* 20 June 1950).

It is peculiar that in the two official American publications about the Korean War—(i) *South to the Naktang North to the Yalu* by Roy E. Appleman, 1961 (ii) *Military Advisers in Korea* : *K.M.A.G. in Peace and War* by Major Robert K. Sawyer, 1962—there is no reference about the capture of *Haeju* on 25th June 1950, by the South Korean forces.

But the *Summary of World Broadcasts,* Part V, *The Far East* dated 4th July published by monitoring service of the B.B.C. reveals the following important piece of news :

"A *Communique* on the situation at 8 A.M. on 26 June (Seoul 09.00-F.B.I.S.) stated that South Korean forces in the Ongjin area had entered Haeju".

This was a broadcast monitored by the U.S. Foreign Broadcast Information Service and may be taken as American official news. Professor Glenn D. Paige noted in his well-documented book : *The Korean Decision* (June 24-30, 1950),

".... American Military Advisers had confirmed the capture by troops of Brigadier General Paik In Yup's First R.O.K. Division of Haeju, capital city of Hwanghae province . . ." (p. 130).

From the first quotation, it should be clear that the South Korean Army launched an attack on *Haeju* on 25/26 June 1950 from the Ongjin area. According to Roy Appleman, the 17th Regiment of R.O.K. Capital Infantry Division under Col. Paik In Yup Co was deployed in the Ongjin Peninsula (See pages 15 and 22). About the battle in the Ongjin area, Appleman says:

"The North Korean attack against the Ongjin Peninsula on the West Coast . . began at 04.00 with a heavy artillery and mortar barrage and small arms fire . . . The ground attack came half an hour later across the Parallel without armored support. It struck the positions held by a battalion of the R.O.K. 17th Regiment commanded by Col. Paik In Yup.

"The Ongjin Peninsula, cut off by water from the rest of South Korea, never had been considered defensible in case of North Korean attack. Before the day ended, plans previously made were executed to evacuate the R.O.K. 17th Regiment. Two LST's from Inch'on joined one already offshore, and on Monday, 26 June, they evacuated Col. Paik In Yup and most of the battalion—in all about 1750 men. The other battalion was completely lost in the early fighting" (p. 22).

From the above statements, we find that North Koreans attacked the Ongjin Peninsula at 4 A.M. on 25 June 1950, and that the Ongjin Peninsula was never considered defensible in case of attack, and before the day ended, plans previously made were executed to evacuate the R.O.K. 17th Regiment. Under the circumstances, we cannot explain the official American Communiqué broadcast from Seoul on 25 June at 09 A.M. to the effect that South Korean forces in the Ongjin area entered *Haeju*, except by assuming that the South Korean onslaught on Haeju from the Ongjin area took place sometime before 4 A.M., 25 June, and that there must have been an element of surprise in this attack.

In Professor Glenn D. Paige's book, we find that Brigadier-General Paik In Yup's first R.O.K. Division captured Haeju, on 25/26 June, 1950. According to Roy Appleman, the different contingents of the First Infantry Division of the R.O.K. Army were posted in June 1950 in the following areas (a) north of the town of Kaesong, (b) at Yonan, some twenty miles westward from Kaesong, (c) at Korangp'or, fifteen air-miles east of Kaesong above the Imjin river, and (b) at Suisak, a few miles north of Seoul (the reserve forces and the head-quarters). A glance at the map of Korea shows that Kaesong, a town adjacent to the border, was a key town in the defence of the South Korean capital Seoul to which it was linked by railway. According to various official and unofficial reports, this strategic South Korean town fell into the hands of the North Korean Army between 09.00 to 09.30 hours on 25 June 1950 Korean time, within about five hours after the north Korean invasion of South Korea started. So the capture of the Northern strategic town of *Haeju* by the South Korean 1st R.O.K. Division contingent deployed north of Kaesong is inconceivable as a counter-attack organised by the R.O.K. forces. It might have taken place only as a surprise offensive, prior to the North Korean invasion. It is more plausible to assume that the two R.O.K. battalions of the 12th regiment (1st R.O.K. Division) posted at Yonan made a joint surprise assault on *Haeju* (synchronising with the South Korean attack on *Haeju* launched from the Ongjin area) in the late hours of the night of 24th June as alleged by the Pyongyang radio, and then came the North Korean offensive all along the Parallel. According to Appleman, "most of the R.O.K. 12th Regiment (First Infantry Division) troops at Kaesong and Yonan were killed or captured. Only two companies of the Regiment escaped and reported to the Division headquarters the next day." (*Op. Cit.* p. 22).

The capture of the North Korean town Haeju by the ill-equipped South Korean forces could not have taken place without an element of surprise and it was bound to have meant heavy casualties for the invaders. All these seem to have been corroborated by the available information. We do not wonder that Chatham House Study Group including a serving British General (Lt. General H. G. Martin) concluded in August 1950 : "Material essential to the refutation of the communist charge that they, the North Koreans, were defending themselves against aggression is still not available" (*Defence In The Cold War*, p. 110).

The Korean War And The Security Council (June 1950)

When the Security Council met on 25th June on the basis of the complaint about the armed attack on the Republic of Korea (South), the Secretary-General said: "The report received from the Commission, as well as reports from other sources in Korea, make it plain that military actions have been undertaken by North Korean forces.... The present situation is a serious one and is a threat to international peace..." We know that the U.N. Commission in its first cablegram to the Secretary-General merely passed on the allegation of South Korean President Syngman Rhee about the North Korean invasion and his denial of the North Korean allegation broadcast by the Pyongyang radio about a South Korean attack across the 38th Parallel. The First complaint about the North Korean attack reached the Secretary-General, as we know, from the U.S. Government who had earlier received a cable from the American Ambassador Muccio in Seoul. The Secretary-General did not mention any other sources in Korea, who might have supplied him with a more objective account of the origin of the Korean war. The British delegate's speech in the Security Council meeting on 25th June is interesting, as it shows that he was not so sure about how the war started in Korea. He said, "The Security Council should not at this moment take action which might go beyond the bounds of the evidence which has been placed at its disposal by its own Commission in Korea. Before proceeding further, it seems to me of primary importance to obtain as full a statement of facts as we can at the earliest moment." The British delegate brought the following amendment, which was accepted by the U.S. delegate: "Request the UN Commission (a) to communicate its fully considered recommendation on the situation with the least possible delay." He, however, did not object to the main resolution sponsored by the USA which noted "with grave concern the armed attack upon the Republic of Korea by forces from North Korea" and directed only the authorities of North Korea "to withdraw forthwith their armed forces to the 38th Parallel". The British position was further clarified by the following report published in the *New York Herald Tribune* on 26th June 1950: "In London, the Foreign Office on Sunday would not comment 'because of lack of Official information reaching London'. It was still waiting for information from Captain Vyvyan Holt, British Minister to Seoul. 'For the time being' the Foreign Office said, 'we are following the American lead'."

The British Prime Minister Attlee said on 27th June, "The scale and intensity of the attack leaves no doubt that this was a full-scale invasion." (*The Times,* 28 June 1950).

Among the members of the Security Council were three non-aligned Powers—India, Egypt and Yugoslavia. Secretary-General Trygve Lie writes in his memoirs, "I believe I may say without risking any offence that my views probably influenced the Indian delegation, as well as the delegate of Egypt, Mahommoud Fawzi Bey, to vote in favour of the resolution which was adopted that Sunday (25th June 1950) afternoon." (*In The Cause Of Peace* : Trygve Lie, p. 329). Egypt, however, retreated to a policy of abstaining on votes of support for the UN action in Korea on 27th June. The Government of India on the other hand issued a *Communiqué* on 29th June 1950, in which they said, "... They are opposed to any attempt to settle international disputes by resort to aggression. For this reason, Sir B. N. Rau on behalf of the Government of India voted in favour of the first resolution of the Security Council. The halting of aggression and the quick restoration of peaceful conditions are essential preludes to a satisfactory settlement. The Government of India, therefore, also accept the second resolution of the Security Council".

The decision of the Government of India in declaring North Korea as the aggressor without an adequate enquiry into the origin of the war on 25th June 1950 was not consistent with the policy of non-alignment professed by India.

WALTER LIPPMANN AND JOHN GUNTHER

Many highly intelligent observers were puzzled by the sweeping advance of the North Korean Army on 25th June 1950, and thought that the North Korean authorities or their patron, the Soviet Union, must have triggered the War. Walter Lippmann commented, ".... Even a comparatively primitive Army needs time to get set, and a large number of people are bound to have been involved in the preparation of this invasion. How then did it happen that our friends in South Korea had no one in North Korea who alerted them, and therefore us, before the invasion started" (*New York Herald Tribune*, 27th June 1950). John Gunther, who was in Tokyo in June 1950 at the Headquarters of General MacArthur as the General's guest, heard from an important member of MacArthur's staff on 25th June that, "A big story has just broken. The South Koreans have attacked North Korea" (*The Riddle of MacArthur*, p. 150). But Gunther dismisses this news saying that the people at the Headquarters were probably "taken in by the blatant, corrosive lies of the North Korean radio". (*Ibid.* p. 151). He was also convinced of the North Korean guilt of aggression merely by the scale of their invasion. ".... on the morning of June 25, the North Koreans launched an attack by no fewer than four divisions, assisted by three constabulary brigades; 70,000 men were committed, and about 70 tanks went into action simultaneously at four different points, while an ambitious amphibious landing was successful. Ask any military man what all this means. To assemble such a force, arm and equip it, have it ready to wheel into pre-calculated action over a wide front with perfect synchronisation on the appointed date, must have taken at least a month." (*Ibid*. p. 151).

GENERAL MACARTHUR'S TWO VERSIONS ABOUT THE NORTH KOREAN INVASION

General MacArthur was appointed by President Truman on 8th July 1950 as the Commander of the Unified Command, which was formed by a Security Council resolution of 7th July. On 14th July, he transmitted to the Security Council through the U.S. Government a report about the military situation in Korea since 25th June 1950, which says: "At 04.00 Korean time on Sunday 25th June 1950, the North Korean Army launched a completely unprovoked invasion of South Korea . . The size of the attack, the fact that it covered the principal areas along the 38th Parallel, and the amount and character of the material involved, and the use of amphibious landings, indicated clearly that the invasion had been carefully planned for long in advance.

"The character and disposition of the Republic of Korea Army indicated that it did not expect this sudden attack. This fact is supported by a report of an Observation Team of the United Nations Commission in Korea, made along the 38th Parallel and dated 24th June 1950. This report stated that its team of observers "had, in the course of a two-week inspection, been left with the impression that the Republican army was organised entirely for defence and (was) in no condition to carry out a large-scale attack against the forces in the North. The observers found that the Republic of Korea forces were disposed in depth all along the 38th Parallel with no concentration of troops at any point, that a large number of the Republic of Korea troops were actively engaged in rounding up guerrillas and were, in any case, entirely lacking in armour, heavy artillery, and air support necessary to carry out an invasion of North Korea. "These facts controverted completely the North Korean broadcast from Pyongyang, late in the morning of 25th June, that the Republic of Korea had initiated an attack across the border and that the North Korean forces had been ordered to repel the attack...."

In this report, General MacArthur also confirmed that on 25th June 1950, the North Korean forces struck southwards in four major drives across the 38th Parallel, two of which were directed towards Ongjin and Kaesong. Also it comes out from this report that the North Korean Army was in control of the Ongjin area on 26th June and that one North Korean division captured Kaesong on the afternoon of 25th June.

He also said, ".... The well-planned attack by the North Korean regime, the size of their force, *their logistical support* and their ability to continue to press the attack, account for the degree of initiative enjoyed by the aggressor. The defenders of the Republic of Korea have been forced to submit to the time and place selected by the aggressor ..." (*U.N. Document,* S/1626).

This report of General MacArthur does not refer at all to the fact of the capture of the North Korean strategic town *Haeju* on 25th June 1950 on the very day of the start of the fighting, though the Republic of Korea (South) officially made this claim on 26th June. He accepted rather uncritically the report of the U.N. Military observers that "The Republic of Korea were disposed in depth all along the 38th Parallel with no concentration of troops at any point .. and were, in any case, entirely lacking in armour, heavy artillery, and air support necessary to carry out an invasion of North Korea".

On 5th May 1951, in the *Joint Senate Committee Hearings*, General MacArthur offered his well-considered analysis about the military debacle which met the South Koreans, and therein he put particular stress on the *"Logistic mistakes of the South Koreans"*. He said, "The South Koreans were no match for them (North Koreans) at all; and the disposition of the South Koreans of their logistic potential was extraordinarily poor. *They have put their supplies and equipments close to the 38th Parallel. They had not developed any positions in depth. Everything between the 38th Parallel and Seoul was their area of depot. When they lost the immediate line, they lost their supplies. They were not able apparently to destroy them en masse; so that at one initial stroke this North Korean Army had a new supply base in the area between the 38th Parallel and Seoul, which enabled them to press south with the full strength of their base being immediately behind them. They no longer had to rely on the long distance from the Yalu to get their supplies down."* (*Military Situation In The Far East*, Part I, p. 231).

It would be clear that General MacArthur's second statement substantially repudiates his first statement submitted to the Security Council on 14th July 1950 on the military situation since the beginning of the war in Korea. We might add that General MacArthur, speaking before the Joint Senate Committee, had no vested interest to hide any fact, since he had already been relieved of his command by President Truman. Anyway, he would not be suffering from any disrepute for the initial debacle of the South Koreans as the Republic of Korea (South) was not within his jurisdiction when the war started, although he maintained a Reportorial Unit in South Korea for his benefit due to the proximity of the country to his Headquarters. He might get away with a prevarication in his report submitted to the Security Council, but would have faced perjury charges if he had stated glaring untruth before the Joint Senate Committee.

General MacArthur's first report also conveys a wrong impression about a surprise element in the North Korean invasion in June 1950. A study of the background of the war in June 1950 would have forewarned anybody concerned about the danger of a full-fledged conflict. The Director of the US Central

Intelligence Agency was able to convince the Senators Bridges and Knowland that they had been "doing a good job" in a private hearing before the Senate Appropriations Committee on 26th June 1950. (*New York Times*, 27th June 1950). General Willoughby, (MacArthur's chief of intelligence) and John Chamberlin in their book *MacArthur*, (1941-1951) quote Tokyo intelligence files to prove that the U.S. Government as well as their protegé the South Korean Government were alerted "that North Korean People's Army will invade South Korea in June (p. 332). They also said, "A substantial portion of the Syngman's army was already physically in position along the Parallel". (p. 334).

The Daily Telegraph published the following despatch from its Washington correspondent on 27th June 1950: "Mr. Chang, Korean Ambassador in Washington, said today that invasion from North Korea had been 'expected for a long time'. He said he had talked to American State Department officials about it two weeks ago when he returned from Korea.

"I told them the need (for arms) was urgent. We knew the North Koreans were preparing and that an attack was imminent".

THE U.N. FIELD OBSERVERS' REPORT

We have already seen that the judgement of the U.N Commission on Korea that the "North Korean regime is carrying out well-planned concerted and full-scale invasion of South Korea" was based on three premises: (a) "the actual progress of operations", and the U.N. Field Observers' report (covering the period 9th June to 23rd June 1950) to the effect that (b) "the South Korean forces were deployed on wholly defensive basis in all sectors of the parallel" and (c) that they were taken completely by surprise (*UN Document S/1507*). But this verdict on the origin of the Korean War completely fails to explain the circumstances as to *how the unprepared South Korean Army*— "deployed on wholly defensive basis"—having withdrawn at the first impact of the Northern invasion to defensive positions, and with their principal defence line along the Imjin river pierced by the evening of 25th June, 1950, could *rally a fairly large concentration of forces that would be essential for the capture* of Haeju, the most strategic centre of population in North Korea near the 38th Parallel on that very date. (According to the Daily Herald correspondent based in Seoul on 25th June, "At nightfall, *Lt. Col. Mahoney, Chief of Staff of U.S. Military Advisory Group,* summed up the situation : all Southern territory west of Imjin river lost to a depth of *at least three* miles inside the border except in the area of the Haeju counter-attack".)

On 29th June 1950, the UN Commission on Korea transmitted the following report from the U.N. Military Observers, *Squadron-Leader Rankin and Major Peach* (both Australian nationals) to the President of the Security Council Sir B. N. Rau, and he placed this document before the Security Council on 30th June 1950:

"General situation along Parallel—principal impression left with observers after their field tour is that South Korea army is organised entirely for defence and is in no condition to carry out attack on large-scale against forces of North. Impression is based upon following main observations:

"1. *South Korea army in all sectors is disposed in depth.* Parallel is guarded on Southern side by small bodies of troops located in scattered outposts together with roving patrol. *There is no concentration of troops and no massing for attack visible at any point.*

"2. At several points North Korean forces are in effective possession of salients on South side of Parallel .... There is no evidence that South Korean forces have taken any steps for, or making any preparation to eject North Korean forces from any of these salients.

"3. Proportion of South Korean forces are actively engaged in rounding up guerilla bands that have infiltrated the mountainous area in the eastern sectors...

"4. So far as equipment of South Korean forces is concerned, in absence of armour, air support and heavy artillery, any action with object of invasion would by any military standards be impossible.

"5. South Korea army does not appear to be in possession of military or other supply that would indicate preparation for large-scale attack. *In particular, there is no sign of any dumping of supplies or ammunition, petrol, oil, lubricant in forward areas* ....

"6. In general, the attitude of South Korean commanders is one of vigilant defence. Their instructions do not go beyond retirement in case of attack upon previously prepared positions.

"7. There is no indication of any extensive reconnaissance being carried out northward by South Korea army nor of any undue excitement or activity at divisional headquarters or regimental levels to suggest preparation for offensive activity....

"8. Observers made special point inquiring what information was coming in regarding situation north of Parallel. In some sectors it had been reported that civilians had recently been removed from area adjoining parallel to north to depths varying from four to eight kilometers... No reports however have been received of any unusual activity on part of North Korean forces that would indicate any impending change in general situation along Parallel".

The U.N. Field Observers' Report (*UN Document S/1518*) has been regarded by many commentators as the basic document relating to the origin of the Korean War. The then Chairman of the Security Council Sir B. N. Rau commented on 30th June 1950, "I think this report is very important, as it bears upon what I may call the very foundation of the action which the Security Council has taken in this matter." The authors of the British *White Paper on Korea*, R. G. Casey in *Friends and Neighbours* (1954) and the late Guy Wint in *What Happened in Korea?* (1954) based their judgment on the origin of the Korean War mainly on this document.

The UN Commission on Korea (1949-50) in their Annual Report (*UN Document* A/1350), submitted to the Security Council on 4th September 1950, said, "The report of the Observers was completed on June 24, 1950, the eve of the invasion from the North, and that the events of the following day conferred upon the observations regarding the defensive positions of the South Korean forces a significance of which the Observers when they drafted their report could not have been aware." The UNCOK added, "This very unawareness gives to their observations a special value which the Commission has taken into consideration", and concluded mainly on the basis of the UN Field Observers' Report and of its own knowledge of the general military situation that "No offensive could possibly have been launched across the Parallel by the Republic of Korea on June 25, 1950", (p. 4; Para 14 and 16).

It is interesting to note about this very important document that—though presented as being "completed on 24 June, 1950, the eve of the invasion from the North", the UN Commission on Korea itself had not seen the *Field Observers' Report* before 26th June 1950, and then this report (which is a brief document in itself), could only be "briefly explained" to the UNCOK on 26th June, 1950—a few hours *after* the Security Council had already passed the first resolution condemning North Korea for armed attack on 25th June 1950. The Report was placed for further consideration by the UNCOK on 29th June 1950. This so-called basic document about the origin of the Korean War was unduly *delayed for inadequate and unconvincing reasons*, and reached the UN Secretariat not before 29th June 1950. Not only that the time of drafting this document is suspect, its contents have been contradicted on major points by General MacArthur's testimony before the *Joint Committee of the U S. Senate* on 5th May 1951, referred to above.

The Record of the U.N. Commission on Korea (1949-50)

We have already noted the major omission on the part of the U.N.C.O.K. in brushing aside as false the North Korean allegation made on 25th June 1950 through the Pyongyong radio about the South Korean assault on Haeju without making any enquiry. The U.N.C.O.K. membership was packed with states (viz. Australia, China (Formosa), El Salvador, France, India, Philippines and Turkey) who were all, with the solitary exception of India, already willynilly tied to the U.S.A. on the issue of Cold War. Even then as an international fact-finding body, their conduct was most unbecoming. While admitting that the tension between the two Koreas continued unabated in the form of border incidents and guerrilla warfare, and appointing U.N. Military Observers for a correct appraisal of the military situation bordering on the 38th Parallel, also noting the intransigence of Syngman Rhee about the efforts of peaceful unification of Korea—together with his frequent outbursts about unifying Korea by force, the U.N.C.O.K. (1949-

50) comes to the curious conclusion that the north Koreans have made an unprovoked invasion on South Korea. And they reached this conclusion without having any first hand knowledge of the situation along the 38th Parallel on 25th June 1950, the UN. Military Observers having left the border on 23rd June—two days before the War broke out.

The U.N.C.O.K. itself brings out the very irresponsible and aggressive nature of the Rhee regime (not to speak of its corrupt and undemocratic administration), which had to be dissuaded from fulfilling Rhee's oft-repeated boast of taking "Pyongyang within three days" by the U.S. restrictions of the munition supplies to only three days' requirements. In these circumstances, it would be clear that any withdrawal of the U.S. restrictions on Syngman Rhee might be sufficient incentive to this Don Quixote dictator of South Korea to launch an offensive against North Korea, eliciting a massive retaliation from the North Korean Government. That there might have been an alteration in the U.S. policy on the Far East since the declaration on 5th and 6th January 1950 by President Truman and U.S. Secretary of State Dean Acheson to the effect that Korea and Formosa were not included in the defence perimeter of the U.S.A., should not have escaped the notice of the U.N.C.O.K. The very appointment of J. F. Dulles as a Special Adviser to the State Department under the pressure of the China Lobby, and the resumption of financial aid to Formosa in April 1950 again under the same influence, imply the negation of the previous policy of the Truman Administration regarding Formosa and Korea as declared officially in January 1950. The visit of Dulles along with Defence Secretary Louis Johnson and Chief of Staff Omar Bradley to Japan for consultations with General MacArthur in June 1950, the visit of Dulles to the 38th Parallel hardly a week before the outbreak of the Korean War, as also Dulles' speech in a somewhat truculent tone in the South Korean Assembly on 19th June 1950, may not be regarded as insignificant incidents in the light of forthcoming events relating to Korea and Formosa. But the U.N.C.O.K. seems to have completely ignored the slightest possibility of any change in the U.S. Policy on the Far East sometime prior to the beginning of the Korean War on 25th June 1950.

It must, however, be said to the credit of the U.N.C.O.K.

that in the first two cablegrams (UN Doc. S/1496 and UN. Doc. S/1503), they merely passed on the information about the invasion supplied by the Republic of Korea (South) without their own comments about the origin of the war. In the first telegram, they merely suggested that the Secretary-General might consider the possibility of bringing the matter to the notice of the Security Council and informed that the Commission would communicate more fully considered recommendation later. In the second telegram, the U.N.C.O.K. simply said "Suggest have Council give consideration either invitation both parties agree on *neutral mediator* either to negotiate peace or *requesting* (?) member Governments undertake immediate mediation" (This cablegram shows that they were quite conscious by then that they themselves could not function as neutral mediators). But their well-considered suggestion was completely ignored by the Security Council on 27th June 1950, when they gave official sanction to the unilateral armed action already ordered by President Truman on the same date. Since then the U.N.C.O.K. acted more as a partisan than as a neutral body and served more or less as the spokesmen of the U.S. Policy in Korea.

YUGOSLAV ABSTENTION AND ITS SIGNIFICANCE

Yugoslavia, the third non-aligned nation serving as member of the Security Council in 1950, played a more cautious role at the time of the beginning of the Korean War. On 25th June, Djuro Nincic of Yugoslavia (alternate delegate) declared that the news and the statements in the Council should cause the gravest concern and arouse the greatest feeling of uneasiness. However, his delegation did not feel that the picture gained so far from the various dispatches, some of them contradictory, and from the statements was sufficiently complete and balanced to enable the Council to pass judgment or assess the final and definite responsibility and guilt of either of the parties involved.

His delegation believed that the Council should do everything in its power to acquire all possible factual knowledge and should therefore hear a representative of the other party concerned, the Government of North Korea, now accused of aggression. That was why he would formally propose such a move.

This did not mean, however, that Yugoslav delegation felt

that in the meantime the Council should remain inactive or should fail to take the action warranted. But instead of adopting a resolution which would assess the guilt of one of the parties, the Council should, for the time being, order or call for a cessation of hostilities and withdrawal of troops, at the same time continuing its investigation. Ninic then submitted a draft resolution to this effect.... Only Yugoslavia voted for its draft resolution, which was rejected by a vote of 6 against, with Egypt, India and Norway abstaining.

"On 27th June 1950, Yugoslavia presented a draft resolution which, Dr Ales Bebler explained, was based on the recognition of the fact that the war in Korea was a direct consequence of the general tension in the postwar world.... commonly known as the "Cold War". He believed that the source of this continued tension lay in the practice of dividing certain geographical areas into spheres of influence or interest.

"The Balkans have been so divided, and the consequence of the policy of division were still poisoning international relations in general.

"Korea and the Korean people were another victim, but here the policy had split asunder a single country and a single nation. It was inevitable that an open conflict should break out between the two sides, each of which was under opposing influences, but it was also obvious that this open conflict added, in its turn, to the seriousness of the general conflict. The United States draft resolution clearly showed where this was leading.

"The policy of spheres of influence has created a vicious circle from which we cannot emerge into the broad highway of the strengthening of peace", Dr Bebler asserted. "Indeed it may well lead us straight into a new world war".

"Yugoslavia believed that the Council should act in a direction opposite to trends followed so far in international relations.

"After only two days of fighting, the Council should not and could not abandon all hope that the two parties involved would at least understand the interests of their own people and of international peace. The Yugoslav draft resolution therefore proposed that the Council should renew its call for cessation of hostilities, drawing attention to the grave consequences of a prolongation of operations. It provided that a procedure of mediation be initiated. The parties should be invited to accept the procedure in principle, and North Korea should be asked to send a representative to Lake Success with powers to participate in mediation." (*Korea and The United Nations* : A United Nations Bulletin Reprint : October 1950, pp. 8 and 11) The Yugoslav proposal calling for mediation was rejected, 7-1.

A despatch from Alastair Cooke published in the *Manchester Guardian* (27th June 1950) shows that "neither frequent telephone calls to Dr Bebler nor the hot persuasions of the Americans and the French could persuade Dr Nincic to go along with the majority". The views expressed by the Yugoslav delegates that the available information was contradictory and not sufficiently clear and that it was impermissible to adopt any decision unilaterally without giving a hearing to the Government of North Korea should have carried a special weight in 1950, since Yugoslavia had already been disowned by the Soviet camp and could not have any fascination for the cause of the North Koreans.

NON-ALIGNED INDIA'S STAND ON THE ORIGIN OF THE WAR

India's association with the Western nations in condemning the North Koreans *in absentia*, though widely resented within India, was largely responsible for convincing large sections of responsible opinion in the West as also in Asia about the North Korean guilt of aggression. Chester Bowles wrote in *Ambassador's* Report (*1954*), *pp. 238-39*, "When the United States first asked the United Nations to take a collective action against the aggression of North Korea, the Indian Cabinet voted to support the proposal ... For the Americans, who take these facts for granted, the immense significance of a firm stand by the Indian Government at the time is hard to appreciate. Throughout India and Asia, the Communists have moved heaven and earth to prove that South Korean troops attacked first. Although they have managed to create considerable confusion, they have failed in their major objective. In my opinion this is largely attributable to the eye-witness report of the Indian representative and the clear-cut position of the Indian Government on the question of who was the aggressor in June 1950. Without these statements, which were accepted by the majority of Asians as authoritative and impartial, the unpopularity of Syngmen Rhee's regime in Asia and the repugnant prospect of white soldiers again fighting Asians on Asian soil might have led millions of Asians to believe the preposterous Communist claim that South Korea had started the War".

Three Indian diplomats, Sir B. N. Rau, Dr Anup Singh and C. Kondapi, were partly instrumental in persuading the Government of India in taking a partisan stand on the question of aggression in Korea. Sir B. N. Rau sided with the Western Powers, when the Security Council passed a resolution on 25th June 1950 in the absence of the Soviet delegate blaming only the North Korean armed forces for the invasion of the Republic of Korea (South), even though it was reported that the South Koreans also had annexed the North Korean strategic town Haeju on the same date. As the President of the Security Council at that time, Sir B. N. Rau also took a peculiar attitude in allowing a delegate of the Republic of Korea (South) to present its case before the Council without extending the same facilities to the Government of North Korea. All these he did without any instruction from our Prime Minister, who was then on his way back to New Delhi from a South-East Asian tour. The authors of the well-documented study : *The Diplomacy of India* : [R. S. Berkes and M. S. Bedi (Standford University Press)] refer to this event as the "....only one weighty exception to India's otherwise constant dedication to hearing both sides as an essential prelude to United Nations action" (p. 94).

In the Indian Press as well as in the American Press, there was provocative publicity about a visit paid by the U.S. Ambassador Loy Henderson to the External Affairs Ministry to meet the Prime Minister and the Secretary-General Sir G. S. Bajpai sometime before the Indian Cabinet met on 29th June 1950. Arthur Crock wrote in the *New York Times* on 4th July 1950, "......Masterful diplomacy by the State Department played an important part ... in persuading Prime Minister Nehru and the Government of India to endorse the second resolution of the U.N. which urged its members to use 'armed force' to repel aggression in South Korea—part of the process of persuading was contributed by Loy W. Henderson, Ambassador of the U.S. to New Delhi." Crocker added, "Also, the Prime Minister's reports from Sir Benegal Rau supported everything that Mr. Henderson had to say."

Apart from these sources, who might have influenced Nehru in arriving at a decision on the issue of the origin of the Korean War and the legality of the Security Council resolution of 27th June 1950, it is possible that Nehru's opinion in this matter was swayed very much by the rapid advance of the North Korean Army. On 7th July 1950, Nehru said in a press conference in New Delhi, "When North Korea launched an invasion on South Korea, it was clear, *without even a great enquiry,* that this was a well-planned and large scale invasion. There had been border incidents and there had been all kinds of charges and counter charges, but the fact of a major and well-planned invasion dominated all that preceded it". A journalist questioned him, "What is your source of information that there was a well-planned aggression against South Korea?" Nehru replied, "The facts are clear enough. You cannot have this thing taking place suddenly without planning and arrangement previously". (*Nehru's Press Conferences, 1950* : Information Services of India).

We do not know what was the exact content of the report sent by C. Kondapi (the Indian Alternate Delegate in the UNCOK) about the origin of the Korean War. [According to Lord Birdwood, the Indian Cabinet's decision in the matter was made after the receipt of a report from C. Kondapi—*A Continent Decides,* p. 203]. Even without the opportunity of going through this official report, we may safely presume that this report was more or less in line with the report of the UNCOK as a whole, since the Annual Report of the U.N. Commission on Korea (1949-50) submitted to the General Assembly on 4th September 1950, under the signature of Dr Anup Singh, represented a common verdict of the members of the commission without any reservation or note of dissent. In my book *Indian Foreign Policy—In Defence of Nation's Interest* (*1956*), p. XI, I made the following comment on the conduct of the Indian members of the UNCOK : "The conduct of the Indian members in the Commission on Korea, C. Kondapi and Dr Anup Singh, should be a matter of public scrutiny as there is ample evidence to indicate that they were guided more by personal prejudices than facts in sending advice about the origin in the Korean War on

June 25, 1950". The late Dr Anup Singh, whom I interviewed in April 1959, admitted that due to inexperience in military matters, also in the context of the rapid advance of the North Korean Army towards Seoul soon after the outbreak of the War on 25th June 1950, and the prevalent opinion among the other members of the UNCOK and that of the UN Military Observers, he was carried away into a common judgement about the guilt of the North Korean aggression.

Nehru, as we know, had also been carried away by reports of the rapid advance of the North Korean Army south of the 38th Parallel on 25th June 1950, and described the advance as "a well-planned and large-scale invasion." But few scholars seem to have noted the fact that Nehru's opinion underwent a radical change by the end of 1955. Dr F. F. Aschinger of *Neu Zurcher Zeitung,* wrote after an interview with Prime Minister Nehru in *Swiss Review of World Affairs,* (March 1956), "Nehru does not interpret the North Korean aggression of 1950 as a mainfestation of Moscow's imperialist world-revolutionary policy. *A thorough study of the documents has convinced him, he said, that the real causes for the Korean conflict must be sought in the policy of Syngman Rhee".*

COMMUNIST CHINA AND THE ORIGIN OF THE KOREAN WAR

Because of geographic proximity and Korea's historic status as a tributary state of the Chinese Empire, also due to Korea's being the bridge-head for the Japanese conquest of China since 1931, Communist China had a paramount interest in the fate of Korea. This fact was completely ignored by President Truman when he ordered armed intervention in the Korean civil war without seeking the path of peaceful resolution of the conflict. A peaceful settlement involved consultation with Korea's next door neighbours—China and the U.S.S.R.—but this would have meant the immediate reversal of the U.S. policy to debar Communist China from entry into the United Nations. On the other hand, President Truman's speech on 27th June 1950 implied that the U.S.S.R. as well as China, the two pillars of 'International Communism' were involved in the armed invasion of South Korea from the North. The American failure to recognise the legitimate Government of mainland China in 1950 was compounded with the denial of the recognition of the paramount interest of China in the security of the Korean peninsula. And that turned Korea into a bitter battleground between the U.S. led U.N. forces and Red China during 1950-53.

Clement R. Attlee (U.K. Prime Minister in 1950) wrote in 1952, "It may well have been that had China been given her seat in the United Nations the Korean War might never have been started..." (Britain And America: Common Aims, Different Opinions in *Foreign Affairs* 1952). Nehru said in the Lok Sabha on September 29, 1954: "I am convinced that there would have been no Korean War if the People's Government of China had been in the United Nations, because the people could have dealt with China across the table." (*J. Nehru* : *India's Foreign Policy,* p. 91). It may be recalled that on 13th July 1950, Nehru had sent identical telegrams to Stalin and U.S. Secretary of State, Dean Acheson, pleading in favour of "the admission of New China in the Security Council and the return of the U.S.S.R.... to bring the Korean conflict to a peaceful solution." Walter Lippman commented on this peace initiative, "Nehru—who through his brilliant Ambassador in Peiping (Panikkar) is sure to be better informed than we are—has insisted that the recognition of Red China is essential to the Korean settlement... His coupling of China with Korea is a recognition of the deeper and lasting reality of the matter, which is that the Chinese interest in Korea is greater than that of any other foreign power". (*N.Y. Herald Tribune,* 28th August 1950). Leaving aside the overwhelming importance of China as an objective reality influencing Korea's destiny, let us see if any evidence is available about China's guilt for the outbreak of the Korean War.

Harrison E. Salisbury writes in his book *The Coming War between Russia and China* (1969): "North Korea was for practical purposes a dependency of Moscow. It had been so created; it so continued. Communist China did not come into formal existence until October 1949. It did not even send an Ambassador to North Korea until August 1950, two months after the war broke out" (p. 96). He adds, "The likelihood is that Korea caught Peking as much by surprise as did Washington. China was not at the stage in the tidying up of her revolution which called for taking on Korea and the risks which might follow. The Chinese were not in intimate touch with the Korean situation. They had no apparatus in Korea; everything was in the hands of the Russians. They had great problems of their own —the extension and consolidation of their regime in China, the conquest and absorption of Tibet (a very major problem) and, beyond that, one which loomed far larger to them, the tackling of Formosa and Chiang, still not protected by any guarantee or any military forces of the United States. Korea could hardly have appealed to the Chinese as a logical or attractive initiative in the spring of 1950." (p. 96.)

C. P. Fitzgerald wrote in *Revolution in China* (1952), "The Chinese Communists had little to do with North Korea. That satellite State had been created by the Russians when Japan surrendered; it came into existence *de facto* long before the Chinese Communists came to power..." (p. 219). He wrote further, "When North Korea invaded the South, alleging a previous South Korean infringement of the 38th Parallel, Peking supported this claim, which the West had rejected as a fiction, and gave verbal encouragement to North Korea. No Chinese armed support was given, and the Peking propaganda department was not prepared for the invasion and did not get its directions for nearly twenty-four hours... The disarray of the Chinese Communist Press during the first twenty-four hours of the Korean War is an interesting and suggestive fact". (p. 220).

Professor S. R. Schram in his biography of *Mao Tse-tung* also dismisses the view of the people who blamed Chinese bellicosity for the North Korean invasion of South Korea. "The civil war was still not over; isolated pockets of resistance remained to be wiped out in various remote provinces; control had not yet been established in Tibet; and, above all, Mao was resolved to defeat the remnants of Chiang's forces on Taiwan. Troops for this purpose were poised in the adjoining forces, and there is clear evidence that the invasion was planned for the summer." (p. 262).

K. M. Panikkar, the Indian Ambassador in China, wrote about the Chinese reaction at the beginning of the Korean War, "U.N. intervention in Korea caused no particular reaction in China: in fact during the first three months of the Korean War there was hardly any noticeable military activity in China. But the (U.S.) intervention in Taiwan was considered to be a direct threat, though even in this matter the Chinese behaved with exemplary patience and restraint". (*In Two Chinas*, p. 103).

A. S. Whiting wrote in his well-documented study *China Crosses the Yalu*, "There is little evidence...that the Chinese commitments in North Korea compared in any way with those of the Soviet Union. In particular, there is no clear evidence of Chinese participation in the planning and preparation of the Korean War". (p. 45).

In the Blair House meeting in Washington on 25th June 1950, where President Truman and his top Advisers gathered, the prevalent feeling was that China was at the time poised for an attack on Formosa than Korea. Professor Glenn D. Paige writes, "The Conferees believed that the plans of the Chinese Communists to invade Formosa were still in effect. Intelligence reports indicated that they had completed their invasion preparation by June 15. (*The New York Times*, 28 June 1950, Hanson Baldwin). Secretary Johnson had information that a build-up of Communist forces on the mainland opposite the island, from slightly over 40,000 to about 156,000 had coincided with his two-week trip to the Far East. (*Hearings, Part IV*, 2621)" [*See The Korean Decision*, p. 133].

In his article *How the Korean decision was made*, Albert L. Warner wrote the following referring to the discussions held at the Blair House on 26th June 1950, "... What Russia would do when we began to employ our armed forces was considered. The general belief was that Russia would not intervene with its own forces. *What China would do—got very little consideration.*" (*Harper's Magazine* : June 1951, p. 103).

It should be clear from the available material that Communist China's involvement in the origin of the Korean War was minimal.

Conflicting Theories About The Origin of the Korean War

As we pointed out at the outset, no attempt has yet been made for a factual study of the origin of the Korean War on 25th June 1950. Each side relied mainly on circumstantial evidence to put the blame on the other side. The pet theory widely prevalent in the West is that the Korean War was an example of Soviet armed 'aggression by proxy' (*The Economist*) : "There has also been speculation that the time table of the North Korean invasion was settled during Stalin-Mao conversations in Moscow prior to the signing of the Sino-Soviet Agreement in February 1950, which was occasioned primarily by the common fear of the revival of Japanese militarism with American backing. But most of the scholars dismiss the view that Mao had any premonition about outbreak of the war" (A S. Whiting, Edgar Snow, Harrison Salisbury, Harold C. Hinton etc.). In *Khrushchev Remembers,* (a book whose authorship is doubtful), it is claimed that Kim Il-Sung of North Korea came to Moscow and got Stalin's permission to attack the south. (pp. 367-68). It is also claimed in that book that Stalin decided to ask Mao Tse-tung's opinion about Ki Il-Sung's suggestion and that Mao Tse-tung also answered affirmatively (p. 368). Edgar Snow notes in his book *Other Side of the River,* "It is often observed that Korea provided an Asian diversion from Russia's difficulties in countering Western pressure in Europe. Cynics have gone further to suggest that the whole Korean venture was Stalin's design to bring the United States into irreconcilable conflict with China. That probably credits Stalin with greater Machiavellian cunning than any one man can possess". (p. 654) In a closely argued article, viz., *North Korea Jumps The Gun* in *Current History,* March 1951, Wilbur Hitchcock, who was a member of the American Military Government 1945-48, examines the various arguments in favour of the theory of Soviet responsibility for triggering the Korean War in detail. But he finds no rational explanation for a Soviet adventure in Korea and comes to the conclusion that the invasion of South Korea was ordered by Premier Kim Il-Sung of North Korea, not only without instructions from Moscow but without its knowledge. I. F. Stone in his book *Hidden History of the Korean War* (pp. 62-63) quotes the testimony of a Russian Colonel, who fled from the Soviet zone of Germany in the summer of 1949, which shows that the Russian Politbureau refused to give an air force to the North Korean Communist party lest they create mischief in the Far East. Professor Max Beloff in his well-documented study, *Soviet Policy in the Far East* (p. 255), wrote, "It has been seen that there are a number of important events for which such (i.e. direct) Soviet responsibility cannot be proved—among them the outbreak of the Korean War."

Edgar Snow wrote in 1962, "To this day the Peking Government maintains—and most of the people of China seem to believe—that South Korea began the attack at American instigation. I have seen no convincing proof of that, I do not believe it, and most of the world does not believe it. (If it should ever be proved, more than a decade of history would have to be completely rewritten). But it should not be overlooked that the foolish Syngman Rhee and his generals did repeatedly threaten, and appealed for American support of, an armed conquest of the North." (*Op. Cit.* p. 714).

DYNAMICS OF THE KOREAN POLITICS AND THE POLICIES OF SYNGMAN RHEE

We have seen that the U.N. Commission on Korea never tried to verify the charge of South Korean invasion of North Korea on the Haeju area which they heard at 1.35 P.M. on 25th June 1950. They called the North Korean invasion "a war of aggression, without provocation, and without warning". (*Report of the UN Commission on Korea* 1949-50 : *U.N. Doc.* A/1350 p. 4). Without proper scrutiny, they concluded that the North Korean appeals for peaceful unification in early June 1950 in the context of the debacle faced by Syngman Rhee's party in May 30 elections were but fake appeals to serve as a cover for their designs of aggression. They did not at all feel it necessary to probe into the possibility of a provocation from the South Korean side, forgetting conveniently the fact of artificial partition of Korea and past border skirmishes and recent tense situation along the border following the arrest of the three peace emissaries from North Korea near the border. They forgot how Syngman Rhee, who manipulated a monopoly of power and patronage through the mechanism of a Presidential Constitution since 1948, was facing increasing challenge from the South Korean Assembly which wanted to revise the Constitution so as to make the Cabinet responsible to the Legislature, and that the debacle of Rhee's party in the recent elections foreboded ill for Rhee's political future. It was in this context that J. F. Dulles paid a three-day visit to Korea, on a SOS call sent by Syngman Rhee through his

Ambassador John Myung Chang, who had returned from Seoul in the second week of June 1950. (Homer Bigart's report in *N.Y. Herald Tribune*, 26 June 1950). Many intelligent observers of the Korean scene in 1950 had marked how the South Korean Republic was turning into a police state under Syngman Rhee, how Rhee was trying to defer Assembly elections due in May 1950 by six months by raising the alibi of an invasion from the North, and failed to take measures to check the inflationary pressures. In January 1950, the U.S. Roving Ambassador Jessup during his visit to Seoul found that "many opposition deputies were either in jail or out on bail" (George M. McCune : *Korea To-day*, 1950, p. 244), and "indicated American dissatisfaction with severe restraints the Government had recently imposed upon civil rights." (*Ibid.*, p. 244). In an *aide memoire* in April 1950, the U.S. Secretary of State, Dean Acheson, threatened to review the Korean aid programme unless anti-inflationary measures were forthcoming, and expressed concern regarding Rhee's intention of postponing elections. "It was only after such threat that taxes were raised as an anti-inflationary measure, and elections were held on schedule." (Richard C. Allen : *Korea's Syngman Rhee*, (1960), p. 117).

The desperate position of Syngman Rhee in June 1950 after the elections will be made clear from the following quotation : "Rhee was, in fact, not at all anxious to hold elections. He had split with the Korean Democratic Party the previous year over issues of patronage after the group charged him with ingratitude for the support it had given him for the presidency. In late 1949, Assembly Speaker P.H. Shinicky and one-time National Police Director Cho Byongok had merged the K.D.P. with other conservative elements to form the anti-Rhee Democratic National Party. In the Assembly the new party called for a constitutional amendment to make the Cabinet responsible to the Assembly, and in general moved to curb the power of the presidency. Independents on the political scene, appalled by the excesses of Rhee's campaign against the domestic Left, tended to favour some check on the executive. A major fight was in the prospect.

"The first skirmishes went to Rhee's opponents. When elections were held on May 30, the result was a resounding defeat for the Administration. Rhee's following in the Assembly

dropped from fifty-six to twelve, even including the pro-Administration Independents he could count on only about sixty-five votes. Almost immediately the Democratic Nationalists set about introducing a measure to make the Cabinet responsible to the National Assembly." (Richard C. Allen: *Ibid*, pp. 117-18).*
In this political context of South Korea, the appeals from North Korea on June 19 that the North Korean Legislature and the South Korean National Assembly should jointly organise a single All-Korea Assembly to draft a Constitution for the whole of Korea were not to be brushed aside as dishonest. (The U.N. Commission on Korea, however, in their report made the unwarranted statement, "The radio propaganda offensive calling for early unification by peaceful means seems to have been intended solely for the screening effect." (*U.N. Doc.* S/1505). On 20th June 1950, the Swiss paper the *Neue Zurrcher Zeitung* published the following report from Seoul by its Far East correspondent : "In Southern Korea there is no shortage of people who see a solution for the serious economic problem in an armed attack on the North. The well-trained, American equipped Army, numbering 1,,00,000 men, to which should be added police detachments numbering 50,000 men, will most likely be considerably superior to the North Korean Army."

Apart from the autocratic inclinations of Syngman Rhee, the U.S. Government was aware of the fact that Syngman Rhee had been ardently eager to attain a forcible unification of Korea since the inauguration of the Republic of Korea (South) in August 1948. (Rhee might claim to have received the blessings of General MacArthur, who speaking in Seoul at the inauguration ceremony of the Republic, said of the 38th Parallel, "This barrier must be and will be torn down. Nothing shall prevent the ulti-

---

* *The Manchester Guardian* published on 3 August, 1950, an article entitled *The Two Koreas* written by its Special Correspondent. This contains the following comments on the Rhee regime : "Dr. Rhee's administration was based on the police state system. The peasants were treated ruthlessly, the opposition persecuted, leading opposition papers were closed and their editors arrested, and the graft and corruption that was on inside the country gave it a close resemblance to one of the Central American "Banana Republics".

"The election in May caused a considerable loss of Dr. Rhee's prestige, and there is no doubt that the new Assembly was determined to strip him of many of his dictatorial powers."

mate unity of your people as free men of a free nation" (John Gunthur : *The Riddle of MacArthur*, pp. 154-55). President Rhee alarmed some American officials with the talk of invading North Korea, such as in a comment to Secretary of the Army, Kenneth C. Royall, in February 1949. (See Glenn D. Paige *Op. Cit.*, p. 69). At a Press Conference held in Seoul on the 30th December 1949, Syngman Rhee said, "In the new year we shall all strive as one man to regain the lost territory. Upto now, in view of the international situation we have pursued a peaceful policy corresponding to the peaceful policy of the United States and the United Nations. We must remember, however, that in the new year, in accordance with the changed international situation, it is our duty *to unify Southern and Northern Korea by our own strength.*" In January 1950, General Roberts, Chief of the U.S. Korean Military Advisory Group, stated to the members of the U.N. Commission that "the Government of the United States had informed the Government of the Republic that the launching of army attack from South Korea would be immediately followed by the termination of all aid, both military and economic, from the United States. Further, he stated that armament left to the Army of the Republic of Korea by the United States forces when they withdrew had been limited to defensive weapons, including small calibre artillery, but without tanks and without airplanes, and that this had been done in order to make it impossible for South Korea even to contemplate launching a war of unification of the country" (*U.N. Doc. S*/1350, p. 10).

In February 1950, Syngman Rhee with the Chief of his Army paid a visit to General MacArthur in Tokyo. On 1 March 1950, Syngman Rhee again made a provocative speech. *The New York Times* published a report from its Seoul correspondent on 2nd March 1950 under the caption :

Rhee Promises Aid To the North Koreans
Hints Use Of Force Against "Foreign Puppets."

The *Manchester Guardian* (2nd March, 1950) published a Reuter message from Seoul under the caption :

President's Strong Speech : *Hope Of Uniting Korea.*

"Observers here believe Dr. Rhee gained confidence from his recent talks with General MacArthur. His speech is the strongest he has made since the American troops withdrew last June."

On 14th March 1950, *The New York Times* published a report from Walter Sullivan, its Seoul Correspondent, to the effect that "13 members of South Korean National Assembly ... were found guilty to-day on charges of violating the National Security Act and sentenced to prison terms ranging from $1\frac{1}{2}$ to 10 years." Among the charges levelled against them, he reported, was the one of "opposing the invasion of North Korea by South Korean forces." Another *New York Times* correspondent, Richard J. A. Johnson, who had spent some years in South Korea told a Press Club audience in New York on 27 April 1950, ".... there is a very real desire on the part of South Koreans to attack North Korea, restrained only by the fact the U.S. authorities allow them only enough ammunition at a time for three days' fighting." (See D. N. Pritt, *New Light On Korea*).

Willard Shelton wrote in *The Nation* (8 July, 1950), "the Department of State has confirmed the report that he (Syngman Rhee) proposed, several weeks ago, to invade the North and that the project was vetoed by the United States."

Blare Bolles wrote in *The Foreign Policy Bulletin* (14 July, 1950), "Former South Korean Minister of Home Affairs, Kim Hyo Suk, shifted his allegiance to North Korea after fighting began and on July 5 accused President Rhee of having ordered on July 25 the invasion of North Korea."

In this context, it would not be unreasonable to surmise that the psychological impact on Syngman Rhee of the morale-boosting speech delivered by J. F. Dulles in Seoul on 19 June 1950 might have been disastrous. Ambassador Dulles told the Korean National Assembly that just as the United States had served the world in the nineteenth century, the Republic of Korea could serve the same function in the twentieth century. Referring to the 'Great Korean experiment', he predicted that the "peaceful influences" of a "wholesome society of steadily expanding well being" would eventually disintegrate the hold of Soviet Communism on your fellows to the north and irresistably draw them into unity with you." In the last paragraph, the Ambassador assured the Korean legislators, "You are not alone. You will never be alone so long as you continue to play worthily your part in the great design of human freedom" (Glenn D. Paige, *Op. Cit.* p. 74). Secretary of State Acheson later told Professor Glenn D. Paige in an interview in October 1955 that Dulles made the visit to South Korea on his own and that the draft of the above speech had not been shown to him. "It was a case", he recalled, "when you had a fellow out in the field who wanted to do something and you could not say 'no'." (*Ibid*, p. 74).

THE NEED FOR A REVALUATION OF THE EVIDENCE ON THE ORIGIN OF THE KOREAN WAR

Uptil now, there has not been any serious probe into the possibility that Syngman Rhee might have triggered the Korean war on the basis of factual evidence. The arguments of Sir John Pratt in this respect were inconclusive (*Korea—The Lie That Led To War* : 1951). In his Press conference on 7th July 1950, Nehru implied that without Soviet backing the North Korean invasion could not have been launched. In that delicate phase of the Cold War, it was the Indian verdict about the North Korean guilt for aggression which tilted the balance of world opinion on this issue. But by the end of 1955, Nehru's opinion on the origin of the Korean War underwent a total change on a further study of documents—which, however, remained unspecified in his interview with Dr Aschinger noted above. It has been unfortunate that we did not get the true picture about the military situation during the first hours of fighting along the 38th Parallel, on 24-25 June, 1950, either from the U.N. Commission, its Military Observers, or the published official histories of the Korean War. The general idea has been conveyed that there was an unprovoked aggression from the North all along the Parallel starting from 4 A.M., and that since the South Koreans were but lightly armed, they were forced to fall back in all areas at the first onslaught. But from a study of the facts of 25th June 1950, collected by Professor Glenn D. Paige, it appears that Major Walter Greenwood Jr. K.M.A.G., Deputy Chief of Staff, first learned of the attack at 5-30 A.M. He did not feel sure until three hours later that the North Koreans had launched an attack in an attempt to invade the Republic. It was some eight hours after the North Korean attack had begun, that both the operations and intelligence officers of the K.M.A.G. were agreed that a full-scale invasion was on. Even the position at noon did not apparently create much worry in South Korea. As John C. Caldwell, Deputy Director of the U.S. Information Service in Seoul, later recalled, "nothing but optimism prevailed among the Koreans and optimism was the official tone of the American Embassy" (Glenn D. Paige, *Op. Cit.*, pp. 84-85).

The main combatants of the Korean War, viz., the U.S.A. and the People's Republic of China are now eager to bury the bitter past of their rivalry over the domination of the Far East since 1950. Truth has been the first casualty in War, 'Hot' as well as 'Cold', and this happened in the case of the Korean War as well. It is time that an exhaustive study of the origin of the Korean War should be taken up by an international body of experts to know the whole truth about this major conflict devoid of anomalies and contradictions in the evidence provided by the accounts published so far.

ORIGIN OF THE KOREAN WAR AND INDIA'S STAND

I

It has been the generally accepted view in the West that the war in Korea on 25 June 1950, was precipitated by a Communist aggression. The Government of India committed themselves on the side of the Western nations by giving full moral support in the most crucial conflict in the Cold War without fully apprising themselves of the facts of the situation. In the official Communique on 29 June 1950, the Government of India made it clear that they supported the Security Council resolutions because they thought that North Korea had resorted to 'aggression'. But the procedure of calling a country an aggressor without allowing the accused party to have its say in the matter is absolutely unjustified, and was inconsistent with India's proclaimed policy of detachment in the Cold War. In a speech in Madras on 13 January 1955 (*The Hindu*), Krishna Menon asserted that "no country could be condemned without its presence in any International body since they had to hear the views of both sides." But in June 1950, when the Korean War broke out India joined the Western Powers to debar the North Koreans from the opportunity of a hearing—while the South Koreans were allowed to present their case in the Security Council.

India's association with the Western nations in condemning the North Koreans *in absentia,* though widely resented within India, has been responsible for convincing large sections of responsible opinion in the West specially in the Commonwealth about the North Korean guilt of aggression. Also, much capital has been made of this by the American publicists to justify the precipitate U.S. military intervention in Korea. Chester Bowles writes, "When the United States first asked the United Nations to take a collective action against the aggression of North Korea, the Indian Cabinet voted to support the American proposal.... For the Americans who take these facts for granted, the immense significance of a firm stand by the Indian Government at that time is hard to appreciate. Throughout India and Asia, the Communists have moved heaven and earth to prove that South

Korean troops attacked first. Although they have managed to create considerable confusion, they have failed in their major objective. In my opinion this is largely attributable to the eyewitness report of the Indian representative and the clear-cut position of the Indian Government on the question of who was the aggressor in June, 1950. Without these statements, which were accepted by the majority of Asians as authoritative and impartial, the unpopularity of Syngman Rhee's regime in Asia and the repugnant prospect of white Western soldiers again fighting Asians on Asian soil might have led millions of Asians to believe the preposterous Communist claim that South Korea had started the war." *Ambassador's Report,* pp. 238-39.

Bowles added that "In the judgement of the veteran New York Times reporter in India, Robert Trumbull, these acts represented 'a courageous decision in the context of the delicate state of Indian public opinion.' He reported that Nehru had 'risked offending a large section of the Indian public that is ultrasensitive on the East-West question'."

A well-known British observer of Indian affairs, Lord Birdwood, writes in his book *A Continent Dcides,* p. 202, on the question of India's support to the Security Council resolutions of June 25 and June 27, 1950: "Late in June, 1950, after four days of hesitation, India accepted the two United Nations resolutions by which action was taken to halt aggression in Korea. The acceptance was the more welcome because it had been wisely made after the receipt of a report from C. Kondapi, the Indian delegate on the United Nations Commission on Korea, whose sympathies were known to be by no means with the South Korean administration. The Indian attitude was therefore governed solely by the firm conviction that the North Korean had committed an act of aggression and Nehru felt that the weight of his country's moral conviction should be lent to the cause of the United Nations."

In the context of the above statements, it is pertinent to enquire what was the exact content of the report sent by Kondapi about the origin of the Korean war. Even without having the opportunity of going through this official report, we would safely presume that this report was more or less in line with the report of the U.N. Commission as a whole, since the annual report of the U.N. Commission on Korea submitted to the General Assembly on 4 September 1950, under the signature of the other Indian delegate in the U.N. Commission on Korea, Dr Anup Singh, represented a common verdict of the members of the Commission without any reservation or note of dissent.

In spite of assertions to the contrary, it remains an unchallengeable fact that the U.N. Commission on Korea had no eyewitness account to rely upon, when the war started at the 38th Parallel at dawn on 25 June 1950, with charges and countercharges about aggression alleged by North Korea as well as South Korea, the U.N. Field Observers—of Australian nationality —having left the Parallel on 23 June, two days before the war started. In fact, the conduct of the U.N. Commission on Korea (1949-50) as a whole was most unbecoming, and the Indian delegates on the Commission should share the blame along with other members. While admitting that the tension between the two Korean regimes continued unabated in the form of border incidents and guerrilla warfare, appointing Field Observers for a correct appraisal of the military situation bordering on the 38th Parallel and also noting the intransigence of Syngman Rhee about the peaceful unification of Korea—together with his frequent outbursts about unifying Korea by force—the UNCOK (1949-50) comes to the curious conclusion that the North Koreans made an unprovoked aggression on South Korea,—and this was done without having any firsthand knowledge of the situation at the 38th Parallel on 25 June 1950. An attempt is being made here to represent the facts, which might provide a definite clue to the exact circumstances of the origin of the war in Korea on 25 June 1950.

II

A Study of Facts relating to the Origin of the Korean War—25 June 1950

The Times, 26 June, 1950   —Seoul, Monday, 4 a.m.
"Northern forces are reported by American experts to have captured all territory west of Kinchin (Imjin) river, the only barrier covering Seoul."

The Manchester Guardian, 26 June, 1950 —Seoul, 25 June, 1950
"North Korean troops tonight crossed the river Imjin, the last natural barrier before Seoul, the Southern capital, 35 miles to the South-East.

"The Southerners fell back to the Imjin earlier today when the invaders overran the territory to the west of it—Ongjin peninsula. Apart from Ongjin itself, the largest town captured by the North Korean forces is Kaesung, a railway junction just south of the frontier along the 38th Parallel."

The Daily Telegraph, 26 June, 1950.—Seoul, South Korea, Monday.

'The Communist People's Republic in North Korea launched an attack at dawn yesterday on the Republic of Korea, which comprises the South half of the country.

"The invasion followed charges by the Northern Radio Station at Pyongyang that South Koreans had attacked at three places along the 38th Parallel.

"The Communists soon captured all the area north-west of Imjin river, the only natural barrier covering Seoul, the Southern capital."

From the above reports it would appear that the North Korean army invaded South Korea on 25 June 1950, at some unspecified time and captured the towns of Ongjin and Kaesung as well as all territory in South Korea west or north-west of the Imjin river. These reports seem to verify the statements of the South Korean Foreign Minister and the U.S. Ambassador to the Republic of Korea made to the U.N. Commission on 25 June 1950.

But this is but one side of the picture. What is the other side ? According to U.N. Commission on Korea Report (1950), a radio broadcast from Pyongyang at 1.35 p.m. on 25 June 1950, claimed that South Korea having rejected every Northern proposal for peaceful unification crowned its iniquity by launching an invasion force across the Parallel in the section of Haeju, thus precipitating North Korean counter-attack.

The North Korean claim made at 1.35 p.m. on 25 June 1950, about the South Korean attack on Haeju seems to be firmly corroborated by the following messages published by the British Press :

The Manchester Guardian, June 26, 1950   —Seoul, June 25.

"The American Officials confirmed that the South Korean troops had captured Haeju, five miles inside North Korea, near the West coast."

The Daily Herald, June 26, 1950   —Seoul June 25.

"American military observers said the Southern forces made a successful relieving counter-attack near the west coast, penetrated five miles into the Northern territory and seized the town of Haeju."

The News Chronicle, June 26, 1950   —Seoul, Monday, 4 a.m.

"The South Korean Government claims to have counter-attacked at one point on the border and to have captured Haeju, manufacturing town five miles inside North Korea."

From the British newspaper reports given above, it would appear that Haeju, a North Korean manufacturing town, five miles above the 38th Parallel was captured by South Korean troops on 25 June 1950, as alleged by the North Korean broadcast at 1.35 p.m. noted by the Commission. The U.N. Commission did not care to verify the allegation made by the North Koreans about the attack on Haeju by the Southern forces and just brushed it aside as mere falsehood on the strength of President Rhee's assertion to the contrary. This fact of capture of Haeju on 25 June 1950, on the very day of the outbreak of war by Syngman Rhee's army, cannot, however, be obliterated if we are interested in an objective investigation about the origin of war in Korea.

We may mention another point which seems to corroborate the North Korean version of the origin of the Korean war. The capture of the town Haeju by the South Korean army must have needed a very large concentration of their forces, especially when they had no tanks or armoured vehicles, heavy artillery or air support, which the North Koreans had. Such a heavy concentration of forces by the South Korean army on 25 June 1950, would be physically impossible (*after* the alleged North Korean offensive all along the Parallel), especially between Ongjin and Kaesung, enveloping within the evening of 25 June 1950 all the territory west or north-west of Imjin river—the location of Haeju being midway between Ongjin and Kaesung. The only way that the capture of Haeju on 25 June 1950, by the South Korean forces could be explained from the military point of view seem to be the acceptance of the correctness of the North Korean allegation about the prior attack on Haeju by South Korean forces, before the North Korean counter-offensive all along the Parallel began.

It is very difficult to explain in military terms the capture of the most strategic town of North Korea adjacent to a turbulent border by the lightly-armed South Korean forces, unless they could have taken advantage of some element of surprise.

The large concentration of the Southern forces deployed in the surprise offensive on Haeju, the key town on to Pyongyang on 25 June 1950, must have weakened the defence potential of the South Koreans on the other sectors of the 38th Parallel against a better-armed North Korean counter-offensive.

A CRITIQUE OF U.N. FIELD OBSERVERS' REPORT

We know the verdict of the U.N. Commission on Korea condemning the North Korean for an unprovoked invasion on South Korea was given without any first-hand knowledge of the situation at the 38th Parallel, their military observers having left the border on 23 June—two days before the beginning of the war. The decision of the UNCOK that the "North Korean regime is carrying out well-planned, concerted and full-scale invasion of South Korea" was based on simply "the actual progress of operations" and the negative evidence obtained from the U.N. Field Observers that "the South Korean forces were deployed on wholly defensive basis in all sectors of the Parallel" (UN Doc. S/1507). But this version of the origin of the Korean war completely fails to explain the circumstances as to how the unprepared South Korean army, *deployed on wholly defensive basis,* and withdrawing at the first impact of the Northern invasion to defensive positions, and having their principal defence line along the Imjin river already pierced by the evening of 25 June 1950, could rally on that very date a large concentration of forces that would be necessary to capture Haeju—the most strategic point in North Korea near the 38th Parallel.

The U.N. Field Observers' Report (UN Doc. S/1518) is still quoted as the basic document relating to the origin of the Korean War. This document was placed before the Security Council on 30 June 1950, by the then Chairman of the Security Council, Sir B. N. Rau, who commented: "I think this report is very important. as it bears upon what I may call the very foundation of the action which the Security Council has taken in this matter." Most of the commentators of the West including the British White Paper on Korea, R. G. Casey in *Friends and Neighbours* (1954), and Guy Wint in *What Happened in Korea* (1954), based their judgement on the origin of the Korean war mainly on this document. The UNCOK stresses the point that "The report of the Observers was completed on June 24, 1950, the eve of the invasion from the North", and that "The events of the following day conferred upon the observations regarding the defensive positions of the South Korean forces a significance of which the Observers when they drafted their report could not have been aware." UNCOK said, "This very unawareness give to their observations a special value which the Commission has taken into consideration," and concluded mainly on the basis of this report and of its knowledge of the general military situation that "No offensive could possibly have been launched across the Parallel by the Republic of Korea on June 25, 1950."

It is interesting to note about this very important document that, though presented as being "completed on 24 June 1950, the eve of the invasion from the North", the U.N. Commission itself had not seen the report before 26 June 1950, and then the report (which is a brief document in itself), could only be "briefly explained" to the UNCOK on 26 June 1950—a few hours *after* the Security Council had passed the first resolution condemning North Korea on 25 June 1950. This report was placed for further consideration by the UNCOK on 29 June 1950. This so-called basic document about the origin of the war was unduly delayed for inadequate and unconvincing reasons, and reached the Security Council not before 29 June 1950. Not only is the time of drafting of this document suspect, but also its contents have been contradicted on major points by General MacArthur speaking before the Senate Hearing Committee in May 1951 as well as by General Willoughby, MacArthur's Chief of Intelligence in Tokyo, writing in the *Cosmopolitan* magazine, December 1951 : "The entire South Korean Army had been alerted for weeks and was in position along the 38th Parallel."

According to the U.N. Field Observers' Report, Para. 1 : The South Korean Army in all sectors is disposed in depth.... Para. 5 : The South Korean Army does not appear to be in possession of military or other supply that would indicate preparation for a large-scale attack. In particular, there is no sign of any dumping of supplies or ammunition, petrol, oil, lubricants in forward areas."

This report and the conclusion reached by the UNCOK

mainly on its basis that "No offensive could possibly have been launched across the Parallel by the Republic of Korea on June 25, 1950," is definitely contradicted by the very fact of capture of the Haeju Town in North Korea on 25 June 1950.

General MacArthur, though he had previously joined with the U.N. Commission in explaining the defeat of the South Koreans in their unpreparedness before a full-scale attack in the first report to the Security Council as the head of the Unified Command, provided a more plausible explanation for the military debacle which met the South Koreans. by the "logistic mistakes of the South Koreans" in his evidence before the Joint Committee of the Senate on 5 May 1951.

Gen. MacArthur's statement not only repudiated the substance of the U.N. Field Observers' Report, but also provided a very plausible explanation for the rapid advance of the North Korean Army down the Parallel since the day of the start of the civil war—which led many people including Nehru to conclude "without even a great enquiry that this was a well-planned and large-scale invasion" (Nehru's statement, 7th July, 1950). Also, this was put forward by the U.N. Commission as proof of "a long-premeditated, well-prepared and well-timed invasion".

The People (a Odhams Press weekly Publication in London) rightly challenged the authenticity of the U.N. Field Observers' Report on 2 July 1950 : "The official report on how it all began by 'Field Observers' of the United Nations is quite the woolliest document that has ever been produced on a vital international issue, since it certainly does not prove that the North began it at all."

III

NEED FOR ENQUIRY BY A NEUTRAL COMMISSION

Lord Birdwood, trying to make a balanced analysis of the various gestures made by Indian diplomacy on the Korean issue, made the following suggestive comments : "When we have finished weighing the justice of Nehru's broad indictment that Western Powers take decision affecting vast areas of Asia without understanding the needs and minds of the people, we are still left with a grave contradiction, which requires to be explained. That is the simple fact that while acknowledging the evil intent and nature of North Korean aggression, it does not ever seemed to have occurred to Sir Benegal Rao to question the Soviet denial of North Korean guilt. Some will call this diplomacy, an inevitable evasion through the force of relentless circumstances. Other may crudely regard it as dishonesty. Whatever the verdict, the challenge was never made by the one power in the world which might have forced the issue into the daylight of open discussion and international exposure. Would not that have represented a service worthy of highest statesmanship, even though the immediate results might have been to create yet greater tension ?" (*A Continent Decides,* pp. 204-05). Rather than throw a challenge on an issue of doubtful fact, I think India could render a useful service, in her role as Chairman of a duly constituted Neutral Investigation Commission by probing into the course of the Korean crisis, bringing into light the various cross-currents of Big Power diplomacy including those of their satellites which resulted in the calamity of Korea. It should be clear by now, that the real history of the Korean War remains hidden still, in spite of the patent fact of the North Korean invasion. We have already seen, "Material essential to the refutation of the Communist charge that the North Koreans were defending themselves against aggression is still not available" (*Defence in the Cold War,* p. 110). We are not sure whether the Korean War was merely a 'civil war' (G. D. H. Cole), or an example of Soviet armed "aggression by proxy" (The Economist), or Truman's revelation that "Communism has passed beyond the use of subversion to conquer independent nations, and will now use armed invasion and war." On the contrary, whether the Korean War was the result of the pressure of the China lobby in U.S.A. to find an excuse for the control over Formosa to keep it as a base for future operations against the mainland of China (Sir John Pratt), or the desire of the American armament rackets to secure a plan for an unprecedented armament race to stave off the nightmare of depression, or it was just a plot of Syngman Rhee, the discredited politician of South Korea who was at the point of being shorn of real powers, if not losing his presidency—as a result of the Assembly elections landslide on 6 June, 1950—nobody can say categorically.

"One member of the American E.C.A. Mission in Korea, by name Stanley Earl, resigned as Labour adviser in 1950, saying that 'the American Mission in Korea should have been investigated by Congress in order to expose the weakness of American policy there', and that 'the oppressed South Koreans would have rebelled against the Rhee Government' had not the war broken out" (J. Gunther—p. 172).

Up till now there is no proof available about Russian instigation in starting the Korean War ("It has been seen that there are a number of important events for which 'direct' Soviet responsibility cannot be proved—among them the outbreak of the Korean War"—Max Beloff : *Soviet Policy in the Far East,* p. 255), in spite of such comments by an objective student of U.N. Affairs : "The Soviet Government showed the green light to the North Koreans" (Maclaurin : *United Nations and Power Politics,* p. 219). The Chinese Government did not seem to have any premonition about the North Korean attack (Fitzgerald : *Revolution in China,* p. 220). Whether, again, the American incursion in Korea was a result of moral considerations (Morgenthau) or strategic reasons pure and simple—should be a matter of thorough investigation. The whole conduct of the war including the issues such as indiscriminate bombing of centres of population, use of hideous weapons such as napalm, the Chinese intervention, allegations of germ warfare, treatment of prisoners of war, should come under the purview of the proposed Neutral Investigation Commission. Other problems connected with the development of democratic institutions in Korea, no less than the careers of Syngman Rhee and Kim Il Sung—the heads of divided Koreas, and the last but not least, the activities of the U.N. Commission on Korea should be under close examination. All these investigations, properly conducted under an Indian Chairman, whose personal integrity could not be questioned by any of the Super Powers, might throw revealing light into the cause of international tension—without being used by any of the parties as sensational exposures of the half-truths to further the cause of the Cold War. In the book, *The Hidden History of the Korean War,* (p. XVI), the most exhaustive study as yet available about the origin and conduct of the Korean War, I. F. Stone writes, "I do not think that the truth—in this as in all wars—is to be found in the simplistic propaganda of either side. I believe that in Korea the Big Powers were the victim, among other things, of headstrong satellites itching for a showdown which Washington, Moscow and

Peking had long anticipated but were alike anxious to avoid. There is a certain parallel with Sarajevo, though the parallel is fortunately still incomplete." A thorough case-study of the Korean Crisis, though a post-mortem examination, might be of immense help in diagnosing the disease of the Cold War and relieve tension through the dissemination of the truth, which is one of the first casualties of war—hot as well as cold.

APPENDIX

INDIA'S CHINA WAR *

NEVILLE MAXWELL

Marwell's book "India's China War" is the most comprehensive study of the Sino-Indian border dispute. It is also the most controversial book on the subject—readily available to the Indian readers, published by an enterprising Indian publisher. Authoritative publications on the British legacy of the Northern frontier of India by Professor Alastair Lamb are not easily available in this country. The Government of India has uptil now kept the official records relating to the Northern border of India between 1914-1954 out of the reach of the Indian scholars. Also since 1959, the Historical Division of the External Affairs Ministry tried to propagate a myth that India's northern frontier reaches upto the Kuenlun mountains. India's true border legacy from the British days was thus kept hidden from the public, who were fed on the illusion that India had a clearly defined border and that the Chinese committed a deliberate aggression against India in 1962. Under these circumstances, it was not unexpected that Maxwell's book would subject the public opinion in India to a sort of shock treatment and would rouse indignation and angry comments from many critics. The naming of the book has been unfortunate as the author himself admits that "China had been engaged on ... a gigantic punitive expedition" against India in October 1962. (p. 414).

The book starts with a historical introduction about the evolution of the northern frontier during the days of the British empire. This provides a proper setting to the current Sino-Indian border dispute. On this part, Maxwell has drawn mainly on the authoritative works of Professor Alastair Lamb and Miss Dorothy Woodman based on the study of official papers available in the India Office Library, London. Though no research into the source materials was involved, Maxwell has done a good job in bringing

* Review published in *India To-Day*, January, 1971.

into clear light the true British legacy about the northern frontier. This knowledge is very essential for a proper understanding of the nature of the Sino-Indian border dispute.

Maxwell reaches the conclusion, which is by now familiar to all scholars who have studied Professor Alastair Lamb's careful study, "The China-India Border" (1964), that the whole length of boundary between India and China was left unsettled at the time the British left India in 1947. In the north-west the boundary remained undelimited, as the border-line proposed by the British Government in 1899 to Peking was never accepted by the latter. In the north-east the McMahon Line had secretly been agreed to by the Tibetans; but from the beginning this has been repudiated by the Chinese and was in practice being ignored by Tibet.

Maxwell thinks that the Indian Government under Nehru took certain decisions about border claims in 1950 and 1954, which set them inevitably into a collision course with China. He refers to Nehru's statement in parliament on 20 November 1950, which was categorical in its assertion that—"Map or no map"—the McMahon line is India's boundary in the north-eastern sector. He refers to secret correspondence between G. S. Bajpai and K. M. Panikkar on the desirability or otherwise of raising the issue of the MacMahon line with China which took place in 1952. Panikkar held the view that since India had stated her position, it was left to the Chinese to open the subject if they considered it necessary. Nehru accepted Panikkar's advice and ignored the arguments of Bajpai, who wanted to raise the border question with China in 1952. In 1953-54 again, the Government of India avoided the subject in the Sino-Indian-negotiations, which were limited to Indo-Tibetan trade and pilgrimage. Nehru dictated a memorandum in July 1954 in which he tied the agreement on Tibet to the question of northern boundaries. In this secret document circulated to the ministries concerned, it was said, "both as flowing from our policy and as a consequence of our agreement with China, this frontier should be considered a firm and definite one, which is not open to discussion with any body. A system of checkposts should be spread along this entire frontier. More especially, we should have checkposts in such places as might be considered disputed areas." A new Survey of India map was also circulated at this time showing the whole northern frontier as clearly defined replacing the old official maps which showed the northern frontier extending from Kashmir to Nepal as 'undefined', and the McMahon line as 'undemarcated'.

Maxwell admits that in the four years since Nehru had publicly declared the McMahon line to be India's north-eastern boundary, there had been no demurral from Peking; indeed Chinese acquiescence in the Indian take-over of Tawang in 1951 showed that Peking was not going to make an issue out of the McMahon line. Maxwell then points out, "But .. by ruling that the remaining stretch of the northern borders should be regarded as 'a firm and definite' alignment, 'not open to discussion', Nehru had taken the step which was to transmute a boundary problem into a dispute and the dispute ultimately into a border war." (p. 81)

It was the Tibetan revolt in March 1959 and the consequent flight of the Dalai Lama to India along with many thousand followers to India that suddenly turned the Indo-Tibetan frontier into a live frontier. There were, in fact, very few checkposts on the Indian side of the frontier and the same was true for the Chinese side. Practically the only flash-point along the entire border was Bara-Hoti (Wuje) in the U.P. sector. It appears that in spite of the directive in Nehru's secret memorandum of July 1954 for setting up checkposts in the disputed areas along the northern frontier, this was the only advance post set up between 1954-58. But the Tibetan revolt created an entirely new situation with the Chinese armies in hot pursuit of the Tibetan rebels seeking sanctuary in India, and the Indian army being deployed along the frontier regions in newly-created posts especially in the NEFA region. The clash at Longju on 25 August 1959 was by itself not a major incident, but the concurrent leakage of the news about the Chinese road across the Aksai Chin plateau created a psychosis of fear in India.

But then the boundary dispute and the consequent border war would not have followed automatically. In August and September 1959, Nehru spoke in parliament in the vein that it was a matter for argument as to what part of Aksai Chin belonged to India and what part to China. Also in a secret directive issued on 13 September 1959, Nehru said: ".... The Aksai Chin area has to be left more or less as it is as we have no checkposts there and practically little of access. Any question in relation to it can only be considered when the time arises, in the context of the larger question of the entire border. For the present, we have to put up with the Chinese occupation of this north-eastern sector (of Ladakh) and their road across it." (p. 129)

From the testimony of Karam Singh, the commander of the Indo-Tibetan border force which clashed with the Chinese patrols near the Kongka pass on 21 October 1959, it appears that Mr Sharma, Deputy Director in the Ministry of Home Affairs, gave instruction to establish new checkposts in forward areas on 22 September 1959. (White paper III, p. 14). This shows that the Home Minister Govind Ballav Pant and his officials were flouting the directive of Nehru nonchalantly, and that led to the unfortunate clash at the Kongka pass—which gave rise to bitter indignation against China among the Indian public. Maxwell stresses the drastic effect of the Kongka pass incident on Indian public opinion as well as on Nehru's thinking, but he fails to explain how such a border clash could occur in the context of Nehru's instructions of 13 September 1959. Maxwell rightly criticises Nehru's decision of 7th September 1959 to publish all current exchanges with China. This effectively surrendered to the legislature the executive's power and responsibility to conduct the country's foreign relations (p. 133).

Since November 1959, Nehru took a rigid attitude about India's border claims in the Kashmir sector. The Government of India's note of 4th November, 1959, described with exactitude a boundary putting the whole of Aksai Chin in India, and the Chinese were told that "any person with a knowledge of history ... would appreciate that this traditional and historical frontier of India has been associated with India's culture and tradition for the last two thousand years or so..." (pp. 130-31). In early November 1959, Nehru sent a secret memorandum to key ambassadors abroad which said *inter alia* : "He is ... convinced now that China in the present dispute is only after territorial gains from India and not interested in a settlement based on traditional frontiers; therefore he does not see much chance of a reasonable negotiated settlement of the dispute" (pp. 132-33). This sea-change in Nehru's thinking about India's border claims was very much influenced by Dr S. Gopal who had been sent by Nehru to London to go through the material on India's northern borders in the India Office and Foreign Office archives and make an objective appraisal of historical evidence. "In November 1959 Gopal told Nehru that India's claim to the Aksai Chin area was clearly stronger than China's." What sort of historical evidence, Dr Gopal dug up in London, which would establish Indian claims over the Aksai Chin area, still remains a mystery. No such document is available in the archives of the India Office Library and Records. In the authoritative publication of the Foreign and Political Department of the Government of India (C. U. Aitchison : Treaties, Engagements and Sanads Relating to India and Neighbouring countries, vol. XII), it was said, "The northern as well as the eastern boundary of the Kashmir State is still undefined". Maxwell, however, does not blame Dr Gopal for misrepresenting historical data.

It was since November 1959 that Indian diplomacy was hamstrung—due to a conjuncture of events such as the Tibetan rebellion and its aftermath, as also faulty advice on historical evidence about the border legacy left by the British Raj. The ill-informed public opinion in India was being worked up to a hysterical frenzy by an irresponsible opposition which received support from the Congress back-benchers. The incriminating official notes between India and China being exchanged openly, since Nehru's unfortunate assurance to Parliament on 7th September 1959, turned out to be a major source of continuing tension.

The result was that the summit meeting in New Delhi in April 1960 turned out to be a fiasco. While Chou En-lai proposed "reciprocal acceptance of present actualities in both sectors and constitution of a boundary commission", Nehru was constrained to reject that reasonable proposal. The Government of India also refused to accept the Chinese proposals for freezing the boundaries until some indefinite future when the subject could be discussed more calmly (pp. 158-59). The summit meeting, on which apparently the Chinese had set great store, failed; broken, Nehru said, on the "rock of an entirely different set of *facts.*" There is no doubt that Nehru was ill-advised about the *facts* about the border legacy by the Historical Division of the External Affairs Ministry. Maxwell, however, thinks that the summit meeting broke really on the unyielding refusal of India to give up, modify or hold over her claim to the Aksai Chin territory (p. 169).

From the border stalemate reached in 1960, the 'forward policy' adopted by India to establish her foothold in disputed areas in the border region was but a logical step forward. From beginning to end, Nehru and his colleagues were unwavering in their faith, whatever India herself did along the borders, China would not attack. That was the basic assumption of the forward policy, a military challenge to a militarily far superior neighbour. (p. 179). The Army under General Thimayya as C.O.A.S. pointed out that forward patrolling as called for by the Government would invite a sharp Chinese reaction. The civilians, politicians and officials alike, failed to grasp that logistics defined the capability of the army, and evolved their policies without giving due weight to the possibility of counter-action from the other side (p. 202). So long General Thimayya was in charge of the Army, he refused to implement the forward policy in the absence of the necessary logistic support. Then "Officers responsive to civilian requirements, and ready to ignore the basic precepts of the soldier's craft and override objections based upon them took over at Army H.Q. in mid-1961. Thereafter the Indian Government could hurry on to disaster, insulated from the warnings and protests—which continued to be voiced lower down the military structure." (p. 204). Maxwell's analysis of the origin of the border war in October 1962, more or less, agrees with the verdict of General Maxwell Taylor, Chairman of the Joint Chief of Staff of the U.S. Armed Forces, who said in a Congressional hearing that India was edging forward in disputed territory and actually started the military operation. (New York Times, 19 April 1963). Maxwell provides the best available account of the border war with China based on the study of the Henderson-Brooks report on the conduct of the war. The Henderson-Brooks report traces the roots of the military disaster in 1962 to the 'higher direction of war' and the failure of the senior soldiers, after mid-1961, to resist policies that they knew—or should have known—to be militarily impractical. The responsibility of Kaul, Sen and Thapar for the debacle in NEFA was made clear in the report, although the blame was left tacit.

The decline of Nehru, in personal bearing as well as political stature, was one of the most marked and perhaps saddest consequences of the border war.

The book reveals with a wealth of materials—some of which were kept as official secrets—a sequence of events in Sino-Indian relations which was in the nature of a Greek tragedy. The book raised a storm of controversy in India, but nobody has challenged the authenticity of the official documents quoted by Maxwell. There is no doubt that there has been inept handling of the dispute which was latent in the difficult legacy of undefined frontiers with China, which we inherited from the British. It is time now that the Government of India should release the official files relating to Sino-Indian relations between 1914—1954 and publish the Henderson-Brooks report so that Indian scholars may study in depth what went wrong with our China policy since 1947, and who were responsible for it.

There has been expectation of a thaw in Sino-Indian relations for sometimes past in India. But there is a reference in Maxwell's book to a 'fact'—which if true—will be a standing bar to Sino-Indian rapprochement: 'B. J. Patnaik was given responsibilities in recruiting and training Tibetan refugees for guerrilla action in their homeland.' (p. 440)

HIMALAYAN FRONTIER *

DOROTHY WOODMAN

Dorothy Woodman is well-known commentator on Asian affairs. She, along with her late consort Kingsley Martin, has long been a staunch supporter of anti-colonialism and democratic socialism. She was a friend of Nehru, and has been very close to his daughter. On several occasion she has commented on the Sino-Indian border dispute in the columns of *New Statesman*. In an article on March 9, 1962 entitled "The Smouldering Frontier", she foresaw the danger of a conflagration along the Himalayas from continued stalemate and armed confrontation. She was critical of the anti-Chinese cold war hysteria among some of the erstwhile disciples of Mahatma Gandhi. At the same time, Miss Woodman more or less accepted the validity of the Indian border claims in the NEFA as well as in the Aksai Chin area, and suggested that China should have accepted Nehru's proposal that China be allowed to use the Aksai Chin road for civilian traffic on lease, pending a final settlement of the frontier.

Since then much has happened to intensify the bitterness between India and China. The traumatic experience of the border war in October 1962 and the forging of the Sino-Pak entente since then created a psychosis of fear and suspicion in India, leading her to a frantic search for military security and raising her defence budget from Rs. 300 crores to Rs. 1100 crores between 1959 and 1969. In this context, a serious study of the Himalayan frontier stalemate is urgently called for.

Since the publication of the Officials' Reports on the Sino-Indian Boundary Question by the Government of India in February 1961, a number of scholars have tried to analyse the validity of the conflicting claims to the Himalayan frontiers. Pioneering work has been done by Dr Alastair Lamb in his two books—*The India-China Border* and *The McMahon Line*, Vols. I & II. But his work was not well received in India, where

* Review published in *Frontier*, 7 March, 1970.

public opinion still refuses to accept the bonafides of any academic who finds anything favourable to Chinese claims in the Himalayas. On the other hand, several authors such as Fisher, Rose & Huttenbuk (*Himalayan Battleground*), Francis Watson (*The Frontiers Of China*), Professor G. F. Hudson and Sir Olaf Caroe have been more or less apologists of India in their writings on the subject. In this context, Dorothy Woodman's book, which deals exhaustively with the Himalayan frontiers as they developed historically during the days of the British Raj, is a highly welcome publication. In preparing this well-documented book, she had the advantage of looking through the official records up to 1938 available in the India Office Library, London, as also the private papers of important British officials (such as Sir Charles Bell, Sir R. N. Reid) who had a hand in formulating British India's policy towards the Himalayan frontiers. (In India, scholars are denied access to official papers as old as 1914 relating to the Simla Convention, while the Government of India thought it fit to publish all contemporary official correspondence with China dating from 1954). The Indian intelligentsia has thus been long fed on the illusion that the present Sino-Indian confrontation—as bitter today as the East-West cold war of the early fifties—was the product of a diabolical design of the Chinese Government, coupled with the gullibility of Nehru. It is time they opened their eyes to the realities of the problem, which could be the first step towards devising a path for its peaceful solution.

In Dorothy Woodman's book they would see how a British scholar, dubbed an Indo-phile by the Chinese and who actually started from a belief that India had a cast-iron case in March 1962, has now modified her earlier view after a five-year study of official documents. Miss Woodman says, "Clearly any settlement of the Sino-Indian border involves compromise." Being a geographer by training, she has been able to scrutinise the wide variety of maps published by the Governments of India and China to support their respective claims. While a senior student of Asian affairs like Doak Barnett in *Communist China and Asia* (p. 310) was misled to believe that the Sino-Indian conflict over the Himalayan frontiers originated in Communist China's game of Map-Manship', Miss Woodman finds fault with both sides in this respect. She says, "the innumberable discrepancies in maps might lead the most naive student of cartography to the view that the devil can quote maps to serve his own purpose." (pp. 320-21)

She suggests a possible line of settlement of the dispute based on compromise: "The fact that China accepted the Red Line of the 1914 Simla Tripartite maps in her discussions with Burma, suggests that this might be a starting point in the case of India." (p. 321) On the other hand, she thinks that India should limit her claim in the Aksai Chin sector to the Macartney-Macdonald Line of 1899, then accepted by Sinkiang officials but not endorsed by Nanking. In fact, Miss Woodman has now come to the conclusion that the starting point of a Sino-Indian rapprochement would be the formula supposed to have been suggested by Chou En-lai to Nehru in April 1960. K. P. S. Menon, the Indian diplomat, now in retirement, also commended this formula in his book *The Flying Troika*.

THREE TRAUMAS

Miss Woodman concludes her book thus: "India to-day seems to be the victim of three traumas: Kashmir, the Aksai Chin, and poverty. To try to resolve the first two by vast military expenditure can only divert her funds and energies from the struggle against poverty. India cannot afford to play Russia's war game with China, nor her own war game with Pakistan ... India is, in fact, faced with the alternatives of the Himalayas as one vast radar screen or the initiation of an active foreign policy to re--open talks with Pakistan and China. To settle for the present stalemate is to condone a military active frontier across Asia." (p. 321)

The Indian people should by now be tired of the cold war confrontation with her two immediate neighbours, and it is hoped that the advice of Dorothy Woodman, who has been all these years a champion for India's cause in the United Kingdom, will not fall on deaf ears. She does not make any suggestions as to how India could meaningfully proceed to tackle the problem. Like Mr Nehru, most Indians still believe that even the handing over of the Kashmir valley in a platter to Pakistan on the basis of religious affinities will not make her stop from India-baiting. On the other hand, it may arouse communal passions to a high pitch, undermining the slender structure of secularism on which the Indian Union stands today. This is why Nehru was never amenable to arbitration on the question of Kashmir. Yet, he more than once expressed himself agreeable to reference to international arbitration of the Sino-Indian border dispute. A settlement with China should be given urgent priority. Miss Woodman, however, has not considered the difficulties of mutual suspicion after a decade of hostile confrontation. Border negotiations should be the last item in any proposed Sino-Indian dialogue, as the problem has been complicated by such question as prestige and the like. A start may be made by the two countries ceasing their campaign of calumny and vilification against each other. The re-opening of the mutually beneficial trans-Himalayan trade, stopped by the Government of India's refusal to re-open talks on Tibetan trade in early 1962 on the eve of the expiry of the 1954-62 Agreement should be given urgent consideration. Anyway, Miss Dorothy Woodman has written a thought provoking study, which no student of Indian foreign policy should miss.

INDEX OF NAMES

A

Acheson, Dean, 6, 111, 134, 141, 146, 149
Addis, John, 82
Aitchison, 3, 68, 70, 72-74, 76
Allen, Richard C., 146, 147
Appleman, Roy, 123
Ardagh, John, 23
Archinger, Dr F. F., 140, 150
Attlee, Prime Minister, 126, 141

B

Bajpai, Sir G. S., 14, 29, 138
Baldwin, Hansen, 143
Bao Dai, 102
Barkes, R. S., 138
Bebler, Dr Ales, 136
Bedi, M. S., 138
Beloff, Max, 144, 161
Bigart, Homer, 146
Bolles, Blair, 149
Bradley, General Omar, 138
Byongok Cho, 146
Barooah, Debkanta, 5
Battye, Captain, 69-71
Bey, Mahommoud Fowzi, 126
Betts, U., 93, 139
Birdwood, Lord, 153
Bowles, Chester, 137, 152, 153
Brabourne, Lord, 86
Butler, R. A., 76

C

Caldwell, John C., 150
Caroe, Sir Olaf, 23, 30, 34, 63, 66, 67, 69-71, 76, 85, 86
Casey, R. G., 157
Chao Er-feng, 11
Chang, John Myung, 146
Chen, Yi, 52
Chiang Kai-shek, 4
Chou En-lai, 4, 6, 12, 13, 16, 21, 22, 28, 33, 44-47, 50-52

Cole, G. D. H., 160
Cooke, Alastair, 137
Crock, Arthur, 138
Curzon, Lord, 100

D

Dalai Lama, 8, 46, 51, 55, 67
Dayal, H., 39
Dhondup, Rai Bahadur Norbu, 80, 81
Dutt, S., 29
Dulles, I. F., 117, 122, 134, 145, 149

E

Earl, Stanley, 160
Eden, Anthony, 42

F

Fitzgerald, C. P., 142, 161

G

Gandhi, Indira, 61
Gould, Basil, 72-77, 94, 95
Greenwood, Major Walter, 150
Gross, Leo, 110
Gunther, John, 116, 117, 126, 127, 148, 161

H

Haimendorf, C. von. F., 93
Hardinge, Lord, 67, 68
Hedin, Sven, 27
Henderson, Loy, 138, 139
Himmatsinghji, Major General, 9
Hinton, Harold C., 144
Hitchcock, Wilbur, 144
Ho Chi-Minh, 102
Husain, M.A., 34
Huang Mu-sung, General, 74

J

Jessup, Ambassador, 146
Johnson, K., 134, 143

INDEX OF NAMES

K
Kamath, H. V., 5
Keskar, B. V., 12
Kim Il Sung, 108, 144
Kingdon-Ward Captain, 68-70, 72, 73, 75, 86
Kissinger, Dr, 58
Khera, S. S., 18
Kondapi, C., 138, 139, 153
Korbel, Joseph, 20
Kunzru, Dr H., 43
Kushak, Bakola, 20

L
Lamb, Alastair, 30, 32, 49, 63
Li, T. T., 39
Lightfoot, Captain, 79, 80, 87-89
Linlithgow, Lord, 85, 86, 89, 90
Lin Piao, General, 61
Lonchen Shatra, 82, 87
Lukhangwa, 49
Lautensach, 121
Lie, Trygve, 108, 111, 118, 126
Lippmann, Walter, 126, 141

M
MacArthur, General, 10, 41, 109, 116, 127, 129, 147, 148, 158, 159
Mao Tse-tung, 56, 61, 117, 142, 144
MacMahon, Sir Henry, 62, 67, 69, 82-84, 87, 88, 90
Mahoney, Lt. Col., 120, 131
MacLaurin, 161
MacKinder, 100
Martin, General H. G., 124
Marlampa, Garpon, 20
McCune, George, 146
Maxwell, Neville, 14, 52
Mankekar, D. R., 18
Menon, K. P. S., 30, 31, 33, 53, 67
Menon, Krishna, 42, 52, 53, 59, 60, 63, 64, 152
Morgenthau, H. J., 161
Misra, Brajesh, 56

Muir, Ramsay, 35
Muccio, Ambassador, 118, 125
Mohan Ram, 57
Mills, J. P., 92

N
Nayar, Kuldip, 51, 59
Nihal Singh, Gurumukh, 103
Nincic, Djuro, 135, 137

P
Paige, Glenn D., 120, 122, 123, 143, 148-151
Panchen Lama, 13, 14, 36, 37, 77
Panikkar, K. M., 6-8, 31, 64, 97-104, 141, 142
Pandit, Mrs V. L., 10
Pant, G. B., 51
Parthasarathy, G., 33
Patel, Ballavbhai, 8, 9
Pratt, Sir John, 160
Pritt, D. N., 149

R
Rau, Sir B. N., 108, 115, 126, 138, 139, 157, 160
Reid, Sir Robert, 77, 79, 80, 85, 86
Richardson, H. E., 20, 37, 39, 42, 66, 77, 94
Roberts, General, 148
Rhee, Syngman, 108, 111, 117, 134, 140, 145-149, 153, 160, 161
Robertson, W. S., 44
Roosevelt, James, 49
Royall, Kenneth C., 148

S
Salisbury, Harrison, 144
Sawyer, Major Robert, 122
Schram, S. R., 142
Shelton, Willard, 149
Shiniki, P. H., 146
Snow, Edgar, 144, 145
Stalin, 6, 40, 144
Stone, I. F., 161
Steele, A. T., 32, 48

Sullivan, Walter, 117, 149
Singh, Dr Anup, 138-140, 154
Stevenson, Adlai, 111

T

Taft, Senator, 111
Truman, President, 10, 39, 40, 109, 112, 114, 115, 118, 119, 129, 135, 140, 160
Trumbull, Robert, 153
Twynum, Sir Henry, 66, 86, 89, 90

W

Walton, J. C., 74, 76

'Waqnis', 27
Whiting, A. S., 32, 143, 144
Williamson, F., 68, 70
Wilson, Woodrow, 58
Willoughby, General, 158
Wint, Guy, 49, 157
Woodman, Dorothy, 52, 53
Warner, Albert L., 143

Y

Yup, Col. Paik In, 123

Z

Zachariah, K., 22
Zetland, Lord, 90